Matthew Cisco

My Life at The Mitch:
A Little League Baseball Story

My Life at The Mitch: A Little League Baseball Story

Papereback (pb)
ISBN: 9780578030647

Cover design and artwork by Stephen Earley Jordan II
Cover photo credits: Umpire, Chad Baumgardner; Catcher, Brandon Harmon;
Batting, Chandler Milum; Pitcher, Mason Brubeck; Shortstop, Casey Saunders;
Second base, Dana Maynard; Centerfield, Ryan Edwards.

Matthew Cisco would love to hear from his readers.
Please contact him at LoveTheHerd03@yahoo.com

For Mom
Thank you for washing all my dirty uniforms
And for all the assists that should've been

Foreward

A . Bartlett Giamatti once wrote about baseball, "It breaks your heart. It is designed to break your heart. The game begins in spring, when everything else begins again, and it blossoms in the summer, filling the afternoons and evenings, and then as soon as the chill rains come, it stops and leaves you to face the fall alone."

It's ironic that my favorite baseball quote comes from the man that played such a huge role in banishing my childhood hero, Pete Rose, from the game. It's this quote about baseball that I relate to the most. Baseball to me is more than a game. It is a rite of passage that all fathers should pass along to their sons. Then there are the lucky few that have mothers to pass it along as well.

My dad once told me that baseball is the only game that you can fail at seven out of ten times and still reach the Hall of Fame. I think that goes along with Mr. Giamatti's quote. You are destined to fail in baseball. It will happen to the greatest of major leaguers and to the youngest of little leaguers. Only in baseball is there this level of anticipation. You root for your player knowing the odds are against them succeeding. You can practice foul shots and make yourself into a 90% free throw shooter. You can lift weights, study film and turn yourself into a dominate football player. However, you can take batting practice 8 hours a day, every day of the year, and odds are you are going to fail 70% of the time.

Only in baseball does a crowd of people stop what they are doing more than 250 times a game to see what is going to happen. What could possibly make a crowd do that you ask? The pitch. It's the anticipation of what might happen. It's hoping beyond all hope that your little boy or girl beats the odds and THIS will be the time that they are 30% successful and when that 30% comes there is no better feeling in all of sport. Baseball is a humbling game. It can make the greatest of player look foolish at times. Baseball is a majestic game. It can create heroes that nobody has ever heard of.

How many stories have you heard about a football team or football player in the 20's, 30's or 40's. How many parents and grandparents tell stories of the greats they saw play basketball during the same time period? On the other hand, I can list countless times my dad talked with me about Ted Williams. The greatest hitter there ever was he would say. I can recall my grandfather telling me stories about Babe Ruth or my Uncle Rick Griffith telling me stories about how he once hid a penny in a seat at old Crosley Field in Cincinnati only to return years later to retrieve the very same penny he had left years before. My aunt Jane can talk to you for hours on end about why she feels that Randy Johnson is the greatest pitcher in the game today. My son, who is 13 years old, can sit you down and tell you stories about Josh Gibson. My grandfather said Babe Ruth was the best player ever. My dad said that Ted Williams was the best player ever. I said that Pete Rose was the best player ever and my son, even though he was born over 50 years after he played, will tell you that Josh Gibson was the best player ever even though he was never allowed to play in the major leagues.

Baseball is the fabric of our country. As the years pass things will inevitably change. Our world will become more modernized and we will all grow older but baseball remains young. Baseball is the tie that binds generations together. The older generation will tell you that Jim Brown was the greatest running back. Thirty-something's will tell you that Walter Payton was and the younger crowd might even say Emmitt Smith. That's only three names. With baseball you have a never ending debate about the greats of the game. From Ruth, to Gibson, to Mantle, Mays, Aaron, Rose, Bench, to Walter Johnson, Cy Young, Nolan Ryan, Greg Maddux and the list goes on. It binds fathers with their sons. That's the beauty that only the game of baseball can create.

It is with that passion for the game and that love for my family that inspired me to write this book.

So many things go unnoticed in little league baseball. All of the stories that I share in the book might have been forgotten by many and never heard by others. However, if you played at the beautiful Mitch Stadium or in a league, in the middle of nowhere, in a town no one has ever heard of, I'm sure you will be able to relate to most of what I write about.

I can almost promise you that you will recall while reading this by thinking, "My coach was like that." Or, "I remember we had a kid on my team just like that." The stories involving baseball have remained the same for well over 100 years. It's as if they get passed down from generation to generation with the only difference being the names. Little league baseball is no different. When you coach a team you try to teach the kids as best you can. You draw on knowledge that you have learned over the years and you reflect on mistakes you made in your playing days so you can teach the players not to make the same mistakes. The beauty of baseball is you can be sure that no matter how hard you teach, each and every one of the players will make the very same mistakes.

If taught the right way little league baseball should have their players go out better than what they came in but more importantly should supply these children with a lifetime of memories that they can look back on with great joy.

I've often said that the only time a player in little league should cry on the field is if they are hurt. Be it being hit by a ball or a blow to their pride at the thought of letting their team down in their eyes. That, and only that, should be the only reason for a child to cry on a baseball field. If you as a coach or a parent are making these children cry, then you are doing a huge injustice to them. You will inevitably make them hate to play a game that should bring them nothing but joy. For little league players and all players for that matter, baseball is a copycat game. You as a mother or father can go out and spend $200 on a bat so little "Tommy" can have a better chance of hitting the ball out of the park. Yet, if little "Johnny" hits a home run with the $25 league issued bat you can rest assured that you just wasted $200 of your hard earned money. Guess which bat your kid will use the next time they go to the plate?

Kids will emulate a stance that they see their favorite players do. When I was 9 I used to get in a crouch just like Pete Rose even though I knew I couldn't be less comfortable at that very moment. When I saw Ray Knight on TV hit a homerun when I was 10 years old I thought to myself, "Hmm. Maybe this guy is onto something with that stance of his." I was an upright batter from that point on. Cal Ripken Jr. is known as the "man with a 1,000 stances." So as a coach when you yell, "Get your elbow up Johnny", maybe Johnny feels better with his elbow down. I realize that all coaches try to teach a kid as best they know how but I beg to all that may read this, don't mess with a child's stance. If the kid can hit, trust me, he will hit the ball. Instead, teach them how to grip a bat. Teach them to line their knuckles. Lining the knuckles will add more distance than any goofed up batting stance you want to put a child in. Stop letting kids that weigh 95 pounds bring a bat to the plate that almost matches their weight. And for the love of Pete, stop telling them to "not step in the bucket." 99% of them are going to. Why? THEY DON'T WANT TO GET HIT BY THE BALL! They will grow out of it, trust me.

Just know that regardless of what you do your kid will more than likely not make it to the major leagues. You can buy the big time bats. You can buy the coolest cleats. You can spend ungodly amounts of money on camps and lessons and odds are they will not make it to the pro's. What you can do though is allow them to have fun. Let the children play in the most stress free environment as possible. Teach them lesson's along the way but don't ever be the reason for making a little league player give you "the look." If you kill the love of the game at an early age you are killing that love for later in life when the time comes for that player to pass along the same memories to his child. Who knows, your kid may be the player that millions of fathers talk to their sons about. The odds are against you but it may happen. If they don't make it to the major's then don't ruin the chance for them to debate with their sons about who the greatest to ever play was.

 I started this by citing my most favorite baseball quote. I will finish this off by citing maybe the most important baseball quote of all.

"Baseball was made for kids, and grown-ups only screw it up." ~Major League Baseball Hall of Famer Bob Lemon

My Life at The Mitch: A Little League Baseball Story

Chapter 1

My Playing Days

My 10 year old year in little league. Notice the beef jerky in my lip in honor of Paul Rutherford.

My Life at The Mitch: A Little League Baseball Story

My late father once told me, "Son, don't ever say yes when someone from the little league ask you to do something. If you do, you will be stuck there forever." I assumed he told me this because as a child growing up I vividly remember my Dad constantly at the ball field. He would be coaching my team, dragging the infield or pouring sand on the wet spots to get the field ready for play. My Dad has been gone now for eight years and it's been at least 25 years since he gave his time to little league. What I realized though is that my Dad had built up a mini celebrity status amongst the kids that came through C-K Little League. People that know me and knew my Dad will ask me when I umpire "Are you going to do the 'Big Arn' safe call?" When there was a close call and he thought the runner was safe my Dad would really sell the call he was making. He had this way of hopping that kind of looked like the Blues Brothers dance and would fling his arms over and over signaling that the runner was safe all the while screaming "SAFE, SAFE,SAFE!" My Dad was a student of the game. In my eyes, he was the smartest baseball player to never have made it in the big leagues. What was great about him was that he was able to realize that the game of baseball needed characters in it. From the kids playing, to the coaches coaching and the umpires umpiring all should be rolled into one with their individual characters all lumped together.

It was the spring of 1981 and I was sitting on the bleachers at C-K Little League. The field would later be named "Mitch Stadium" after Elmer Mitchell. He worked tirelessly on the field and was a volunteer for C-K Little League for many years. Mitch even had living quarters in the press box at the field which is where he died. "Mitch" would pass away my ten year old year in little league. I can remember a reporter from the local paper coming down and asking a bunch of us kids what we thought about Mitch. I told him that we should bury Mitch in right field. It was actually a pretty good idea in the mind of a 10 year old boy. Looking back, what surprised me about that the most was that my quote actually made the

12

paper.

"Next up, Matthew Cisco." The gate swung open and I ran to first base. I started playing catch with Paul Rutherford. He was the coach of the Braves. My dad helped him coach that team as well but I knew it was Mr. Rutherford that was the HEAD coach. I kept thinking "Don't drop it, make good throws." I wanted to be on my dad's team so bad but I knew if I didn't have a good tryout Mr. Rutherford wouldn't pick me. He then picked up a bat and hit me 3 ground balls. I snagged them all. I was acing this tryout. I was the best ball player ever to come through C-K. "OK Cisco, head to right field for some pop-ups." OH NO! My worst nightmare had come true. My Dad had practiced pop ups with me using tennis balls but this was with real baseballs. The reason he used tennis balls is because every so often one of the balls had a tendency to bounce off my forehead. This was the highest pop up I had ever seen, even higher than one of "Pop up Joe's", my dad's nickname he gave to Joe Morgan. I knew I had to catch it. By some sort of divine intervention the ball found its way to my glove. I threw it back to Mr. Rutherford on one hop. The next two he hit to me I missed by a combined 15 feet. I blew it. I was going to end up on the Cardinals. I hung my head and held back what tears I could as I walked back to the bleachers.

"You had trouble with those last two didn't ya Bub" said my dad, "I'm not sure if it was enough to impress Mr. Rutherford." I sat in the bleacher for the next two hours while all the other kids finished up. The more I thought about my terrible performance the higher up the bleachers I went. Finally, dad came and got me and took me home. He could see the worry on my face. He knew that I wanted to do good so I could play for his team. "Son, I'm not supposed to tell you this but you were the first pick of the Braves, you made the team." What I didn't find out until later in life was that I was what they call an automatic. Since my dad was a coach on the team I automatically would be placed on that team. Some may say it was cruel to put a young boy through all that anquish but had he not I never would've experienced the elation of earning a spot on my dad's team.

This was back before mandatory playing time. This was when the coaches put the best 9 players on the field and the other kids would play only if it were a blowout. Mr. Rutherford was your typical old school type of coach. He was a tall, thin man with thinning gray hair. He would always have his big wad of Beachnut chew in his mouth. I was always amazed at how far he could shoot that brown spit out of his mouth. When he would speak you could see brown tobacco spit attach to his upper and bottom teeth. To a nine year old boy, he was the coolest. I thought he was so cool I even took beef jerkey and put it behind my lip for my baseball pictures so I would look as cool as Mr. Rutherford. My dad would tell me that chewing tobacco was a nasty habit that a lot of baseball players had, all the while hitting infield to us with a Marlboro sticking out of his mouth. Mr. Rutherford was a hardened man that spent his life working on the railroad yet he never missed a practice. He never said "No" to a kid that wanted an extra round of infield or batting practice. He was always there. He was a strict disciplinarian but never mean to the kids. Once when I was nine I was playing center field. A runner for the other team had slid into second base and hurt himself. He was down for a couple of minutes. It was a hot day so I took it upon myself to get a quick rest. So, I sat down in centerfield while they tended to the kid on the other team. Mr. Rutherford saw this, yelled for me to come to the dugout and benched me for two games because I "disrespected the game." He believed that once you were between the lines you took no time off and acted in a fashion that best represented the game. You ran on and off the field. You ran out every ground ball and pop up. I once took a called third strike and walked back to the dugout. Mr. Rutherford called for time and came over to me. Instead of the comforting I was foolishly expecting I received, "Does Pete Rose cry when he strikes out? No he doesn't because there is no room for crying in baseball." Yes, you heard me right. Mr. Rutherford coined the phrase "There's no crying in baseball" long before the movie "A League of Their Own."

We were a well oiled machine. As the seasons passed Mr. Rutherford grew softer. By the time I was 11 years old we were actually allowed to chatter while we were in the field. "Hey batter batter, hey batter batter, SWING!" Mr. Rutherford, originally, thought that this was a disrespectful act. My dad convinced him that it helped our young minds stay focused on what was going on so he eventually allowed us to do it. I will never forget playing first base and hearing Mr. Rutherford scream for the first time "Let's hear some chatter out there." You can't convince me that our chatter wasn't heard a mile away. We were the only team not allowed to chatter in our league and once he gave the go ahead it was like freeing children and telling them all at once it was okay to scream. If Mr. Rutherford would've only seen what that chatter evolved into when I began coaching he never would've allowed it to happen.

By the time I was twelve years old our league had its best all-star team it had seen in a while. The buzz around town was that this team had the ability to go to the state tournament and maybe even win it. Early on in district play we lost a game. This put us in the loser's bracket and provided an uphill battle to achieve our goal. Bill Pierce was our All-Star coach. He coached for the C-K Reds. The Reds would always beat us out by the narrowest of margins in our league and the league champions coach got to select which All-Star team he wanted to coach. I loved playing for Mr. Rutherford and my dad and I always found it difficult to adjust to someone else's style of coaching. Bill was a good coach, just as intense as Mr. Rutherford but never followed up what he was saying with a lesson that taught us something. So, in my twelve year old mind, I thought he was just mean to us. Later I learned he was a good man it's just that I was used to

15

being taught a certain way. After we had lost in the district Bill decided to "punish" us by holding two-a-day practices until our next game. I did learn one thing from Bill Pierce. My dad always taught me to swing hard enough to make your shoe laces pop. This meant for me to swing as hard as I can. Bill taught me to muster up whatever anger I had in me and take it out on the baseball. "Kill the ball", he would say, "Pretend that ball did something bad to you." While my dad's example and Bill's were basically one in the same, it was Bill's that stuck with me.

One day during batting practice I was up to the plate and Bill was pitching. It had to be 100 degrees easy. I was hot, miserable and having one of the worst batting practices I have ever had. You could tell that Bill was getting upset with my performance as well. He yelled at me and said I was swinging the bat like a little girl and I acted like I wanted to kiss the ball instead of rip the cover off of it. In an act of mock disgust he took his shirt off and threw it to the ground. That's when I saw it. I can only describe it as a dent in his chest. Right smack in the middle of his chest was a dent big enough for a ball to fit in. He challenged me to swing the bat the way he wanted me to and not like a scared little baby. He was challenging me by poking fun of me in front of all my friends on the team. In short, he wanted me to swing angry. Bill toed the rubber, got set, and threw the pitch. By this time I was fuming. He called me names and embarrassed me in front of everyone. I have never swung harder than I did that one time. The pitch was perfect and right down the middle. Those that hit the ball hard and far will tell you that when they hit it they don't feel a thing. This means you hit it on the sweet spot of the bat. Well, I didn't feel a thing. The next thing I see is the ball I just hit sticking in the hole on Bill's chest. He let out this moan and dropped to his knees. I was in shock. I didn't believe what I just saw. Grown up's in the stands and on the field all began laughing. "Be careful what you wish for", joked my dad. However, I quickly realized how miserably hot I was and I began acting all

16

distraught about the pain I just inflicted on my coach. Needless to say, I got out of the rest of practice and sat in the bleachers sipping cold water while everyone else sweat on the field. After that practice our team rallied. We went on to twice beat our rival League 6 in the finals to capture the District title.

I don't really remember much about our state tournament appearance. I have two memories that stick out to me. One is it was played in Nitro, West Virginia. The field was about half a mile away from some kind of factory that made the entire area smell like a dirty armpit. I can remember crossing the bridge on I-64 to get to Nitro and the smell coming into the car. After the third day there we couldn't smell anything. I suppose we got used to it which is why those in Nitro may be offended by reading this. You can't blame them though. They probably can't smell it anymore either. The other memory was of our last game. We were playing Shady Springs. The only reason this game sticks out to me is because my grandmother had promised me $100 if I were to hit a homerun in that game. My last at-bat of the game was against a hard throwing right hander. The first pitch was a curve ball that broke over the inside of the plate for strike one. I remembered that it made my knees buckle and I stepped out of the box a little red faced. My dad yelled, "SET ON THE FASTBALL!" He always taught me to "think fastball" and "adjust to the curve." So I did just that. I guessed fastball and that's what I got right on the outside corner. I swung the bat with everything I had and didn't feel a thing. I trotted towards first base as I watched the ball soar into the air down the right field line. It was the highest ball I had ever hit and I was in the early stages of my Reggie Jackson trot around the bases. As I reached first base I noticed the right fielder was back peddling at full speed toward the right field wall. It was almost as if you could see my smile being erased from my face in slow motion. This inept right fielder, having played my fly ball all wrong, was backing up at full speed instead of turning and running. As he reached the warning track he still had no clue of where he was on the field. Then it happened. SMACK! His back plowed into the wall at full speed. The violence of the impact propelled his left hand backwards into the air where his glove somehow met up with my homerun. He caught it. I was out. Noooooooooooooooooooooooooooooo! We lost the game but more importantly I lost $100 dollars. $100 to a 12 year old boy was like me as an adult hitting the power ball. I can remember the pain on my Granny's face when she told me how proud she was of me. I knew I wouldn't get the $100 anyway because she was a lady of principle. A home run is what she wanted and a robbed homerun does not a homerun make. Instead, she gave me $15 and told me she loved me. Looking back, the "I love you" I got from my granny more than replaced the other $85 I missed out on by not hitting a home run that day.

Chapter 2

Coaching

Me giving Ryan Edwards his usual game day concussion

My Life at The Mitch: A Little League Baseball Story

After my little league playing days came to an end I moved on to Babe Ruth baseball. During Babe Ruth ball I played American Legion and VFW summer ball. There were times in the summer were I would play 5 games a day. I would play one game at C-K Babe Ruth Field and leave there and my dad would drive me 20 minutes away to Huntington to play in a double header for the VFW team. After that my dad would drive me outback in the sticks of Ashland, Kentucky to play a night double header for the American Legion team. All throughout my playing days my dad was my one and only true coach. If my coach had an opinion on something that differed from my dad's, I would listen to my dad. My dad was always hard on me when I played. I didn't appreciate at the time that he was also the one that drove me to all these games. I don't recall a game where I would look in the stands and not see my father there. My dad worked a demanding job at American Car Factory in Huntington. He worked in a steaming hot building painting train cars all day long. He would leave home at 5:30 in the morning and return at 4:30 in the afternoon. It was a job that took a daily toll on him and you could see how drained he was each day he came home. In my selfish, youthful ways I never realized what his day consisted of. He would come home beaten and tired yet never was there a time he said no when I asked if he wanted to go hit me groundballs or have a game of catch.

There would be games that I would go 3 for 3 and have a couple of great plays in the field and I would be feeling real proud of myself. On the drive home my dad would make no mention of how well I did. However he would point out that had I got a better jump on the ball I could've made it a double play instead of just a force out or if I would've hit the inside of first base instead of taking a wide turn I could've turned my single into a double. Looking back I know that my dad was my biggest fan. The time that he put into me, the miles that he put on his old run down cars, the games that he

20

never missed should've been enough to know that he was proud of me and enjoyed watching me play. At the time though, in my mind, it wasn't enough. I just thought he was being hard on me for no reason at all. I would sit there and think to myself "Were you watching the same game I just played in?" After I had time to take in what he said I always found out that he was right. Had I got a better jump it would've been a double play. I hit the inside of the bag and it would've been a double.

Me forcing my baby boy, to no avail, to be a left hander

When my son Jay-Michael was born I had visions of the Hall of Fame dancing in my head. He would be the Cisco that made it to the big leagues. When he was first able to pick up a ball and bat I made sure he did so left handed. He would throw left and bat left if I had anything to say about it. Then when he was about three years old a terrible thing happened. He naturally started doing things right handed. Gone were my visions of the next Sandy Koufax. I can remember growing up as a young boy and hearing my dad tell me stories of how amazing he was. He would always say that left hander's were tougher pitchers and how lefty's had prettier swings than a right hander. This was something that stuck in my mind all those years up until Jay-Michael was born.

When Jay-Michael turned five his mother and I signed him up for T-ball. On game days he and his Papaw, my father, would hop onto his converted riding mower and ride the 6 blocks to the field. My dad got to watch him play for two years before he died. Like my father, I would tell Jay-Michael after a game what all he did wrong. My dad would look at me as if to say, "Take it easy it's just a game". Once I got that look I realized that my dad was apologizing to me in his own little way. From that point forward I realized I would make the game of baseball nothing but fun for my son.

In 1998 a friend of mine, Mick Osburn, began asking me to help him coach his little league team. I had gone to school with Mick my whole life, my dad coached him in little league basketball, and I played baseball with him in high school. As each baseball season neared, his calls would pick up asking me to help him. Finally, in 2000 I went against what my dad warned me about and said "Yes" to little league baseball. This was also the same year I met Dan Brody. He had come down a year or so before me and his two sons Danny and George were on the team. Dan was a laid back type of person that liked the complexities of the game. He was the kind that you liked to just sit down and talk baseball with. Mick was the style of coach that I was comfortable with. He basically coached the way

22

we had been coached. However, his coach in little league was Bill Pierce. Yes, the same Bill Pierce who's chest I stuck a baseball in. When we played, Mick would be the third base coach and Dan would be the first base coach while I sat in the dugout with all the kids. It's during this time that I started to contemplate my decision to help Mick coach. I discovered that boys from the ages of 9-12 have a tendency to be pains in the butt and could get on the nerves of people that weren't their parents. Fortunately for me, we went through a streak of about 2 games where we were getting no offensive production. In the second inning of the third game Dan Brody looked at me and told me to go coach first base and try to change our luck. Well, Dan Brody was Wally Pipp and I was Lou Gehrig because I haven't been in the dugout since. During my first year we had a core of young players that would only get better with age. George Brody swung a big bat as a 9 and 10 year old and you could tell that homerun power was in his future. He would later turn into a very effective pitcher with two basic pitches. A change up and a slow ball. His slow ball was meant to be his fastball but it just didn't have any speed. His change up was an even more drastic drop in velocity. George though, could hit his spots. Any good pitching coach will tell you that it isn't how hard you throw the ball it's where you throw it to. These two pitches help lead George to throw the only recorded perfect game in Mitch Stadium history. Another one of our young stars was Kevin Lawrence. This kid was a five tool little leaguer. He could hit for average, for power, could field really well, excellent base runner and a cannon for an arm. I would tell Kevin during practice that I wanted him to remember his little league coach when he signed his big league contract and get me some good seats. Once I got out of the dugout I started to enjoy my coaching experience a lot more.

During this time my dad was diagnosed with lung cancer. He was still able to get around and would make the trip on his lawn mower to Jay-Michael's minor league game and then hop on over to "The Mitch" and watch me coach my little league team. He loved watching little Kevin Lawrence play. He would often remark on his natural ability and would refer to Kevin by asking me the question, "Bub what's that boy's name that I like so much?" As the year went on dad kept coming to the games. He kept giving me advice in between innings on what to teach the boys. Had people not known he was sick I can almost bet they would've asked him to umpire. I realized that I had accidentally sucked him right back in to little league life. This time though he got to enjoy it from the stands. We kept winning game after game after game. Our kids were learning the fundamentals of the game and learning game situations. While their baseball I.Q. was growing Dan's sanity seemed to be slipping. Like I said, Dan was a baseball guy. He knew not to jinx a good thing so he never asked me to go back in the dugout. Instead, he took one for the team and a little league dynasty was born. As each game passed Dan's temper would increase. A kid boots a ground ball, Dan slams a scorebook against his bucket. A kid drops a pop up, Dan kicks the cooler across the dugout floor. A kid takes a called third strike right down the middle, Dan slams his peanuts in disgust. By the time the season was almost over Dan's voice had reached a level that only a passing jetliner could match. Over the years I would hear complaints from parents about Dan's behavior. What all these parents failed to realize was that it was their kids that made him act this way. Dan would always seem to single one kid out to vent all his frustration on. I can list them all up to present day. The first victim was Seth Adams, then there was Brian Watts, then Casey Saunders. Brian seemed lost at all the things Dan was telling him so it didn't bother him. Casey was immune to it because he was a first baseman. I was a first baseman so I took a special liking to Casey. I informed Casey during his 10 year old year that the only person he was to listen to was me. If Mick or Dan got on him for something I told him to let it go in one ear and out the other. He was to do what I said and what I said only. That seemed to help him distract the constant criticism that came his way be it his fault or not. Back to Seth though, he was the first in the four year generation of little league to catch the wrath of Dan Brody. He took the full force of it and I didn't have a solution at the time to help him cope with it. Seth never realized that he played a huge role in the future draft picks of the C-K Braves.

I began to realize that while we had a good team that would win the league title almost yearly our team lacked characters. Baseball was meant to have characters. Rick Dempsy running on the tarp during a rain delay acting like Babe Ruth, Jose Rijo drenching fans with his super soaker in between innings, Tom Browning sitting in the stands with Cub fans when the Reds were playing at Wrigley and then there is Jake Adams. Jake was the younger brother of Seth so he was an automatic for the team. He was a portly little boy and if you looked hard enough you could see that he had some talent if only he would work at it. Jake was the first on my list of "favorite players" over the years. He was the complete opposite of his older brother. When Jake arrived to our team I think it only seemed natural to Dan for him to pass his wrath on down from Seth and lay it on Jake's shoulders. While Seth would try his hardest not to make a mistake or not act up in the dugout Jake would do the opposite. Now when Jake was on the field he would always try his best. Like all little leaguers though, he was bound to make mistakes along the way. One of Dan's favorite things to yell is "Don't drop bats!" It was because of Jake Adams that this phrase became known. A bat was dropped one day and Dan calmly pointed out to the kids to not drop the bats. He educated them on the expense that the league and individual parents paid for these bats. I felt he made a good argument. I understood what he was saying and told the boys to be more careful. Jake however was a different story. His turn came in the line-up, he grabbed a bat and dropped it. "Guys", Dan said in a slightly annoyed voice," I told you to be careful with those bats." Jake took his place at the plate, struck out, came back to the dugout and placed his bat against the bat rack. PING! The bat fell to the ground. "DON'T DROP BATS!" Dan yelled. Thus a legend was born. At least once a game from that point forward Jake would drop a bat. I knew from then on that every four years I needed to talk Mick into drafting a kid that would drive Dan crazy. Dan can also be credited with making the phrase "Hum Baby" and "Holy Cow" famous around the C-K area.

Throughout my second year as a little league coach my dad would continue to come to the games that I coached and the minor league games that Jay-Michael played in. However he wasn't driving the lawn mower any more. My mother would bring him to the games now. The cancer was finally starting to take a toll on him. His once majestic frame in my eyes was widdling down to a frail, sick man. At the start of that second year Paul Billups, the President of C-K little league, bestowed the honor on my father of throwing out the first pitch of the year. I will talk about Paul a little more in detail later on. It was a sight that really touched my soul. My father was on the mound with little Jay-Michael standing next to him as he threw out the first pitch. It's funny what the game of baseball can teach someone. Each person learns something different. That day it taught me about the love I had for my father. All of those years of him driving me from game to game. All of those years of him playing catch with me. All of those years I would walk by a ball field and see my dad in his car dragging the infield. I learned that day that I really loved that man. I knew his time was coming to an end and I only wished that I could go back in time to those memories and re-live them just one more time.

I could see that dad was deteriorating a little bit with each passing day. I can remember his last game that he saw me coach. Dad's favorite player was pitching, Kevin Lawrence. Kevin had a "rough" inning where he gave up ONE run. I leaned up against the fence in between innings and talked with dad just like I had always done. His words were, "That kid sucks, you need to take him out of the game." I knew if dad were in his right state of mind he would never say such a thing. If Kevin had a good or bad game it was the way he played the game that dad liked. Dad passed away about a month later, May 12th 2001.

Wouldn't you know it that Dad's funeral was on a game day. I got to the church about two hours early and sat in the hallway afraid to go inside. I didn't want to see my father that way. I saw my sister who had been inside and I asked her what dad looked like. She said simply, "He looks like dad." I opened the door to walk into the church and I saw a young boy with a baseball jersey on. It was a player off my team, Tyler Edwards. He was there with his father to pay their respects. I thought that was the sweetest gesture I could ever witness. Little did I know there would be more. I was proud of myself for holding strong so far through the day. I was even cracking jokes with my sister about the people that were inside of the church and how they all had tissue balls stuck to their face from crying. About 10 minutes before the service was scheduled to begin, Jay-Michael's mom said to me, "I think you need to go look outside." She couldn't bring herself to tell me what she had seen. I walked out of the church and down the stairs to the doorway. There standing on both sides outside of the door were most of my boys on my team and parents included. Each of the boys dressed in full uniform and each of them placed their hats on their hearts as people walked through them. I held it together long enough to thank each one of them and kiss each one on the head. I walked back to the church and began crying and couldn't stop. It wasn't cries of pain or hurt but of something beautiful. What these boys did was an act that was put in motion some 20 years ago when my dad coached me. What my dad taught me later in life when he looked at me for correcting Jay-Michael after a game and that style of coaching that I adopted after that moment all lead to this happening. My dad and baseball were responsible for one of my most cherished moments.

After the funeral we drove out to the local cemetery for dad's burial. I was driving in his car with the rest of my family and along the way dad's horn went off. I had bought him a car horn that played the fight song of Marshall University the Christmas prior to his passing. About halfway to the cemetery "We are the Sons of Marshall" starts blaring from underneath his hood without me hitting the button. What was supposed to be a sad day for me turned into a day of celebration made easier by what my dad had taught me and his jokes from beyond like getting the horn to play. After the burial I didn't want to be surrounded by a bunch of sadness. I looked at my clock and realized that our game was still going on. When I pulled up to the field I saw that we were in the second inning. I walked along the bleachers and people just looked at me. None of them said anything. I walked into the dugout and the kids were the first to see me and they too didn't say anything. Then Dan Brody looked and saw me and walked the length of the dugout and gave me a hug. He told me that he was sorry for my loss and that my dad wouldn't want me to be any place else. My opinion of Dan Brody changed that very second and I would later defend him against any attack that would come from any little league parent.

I would have to say that the best coaching trait my father passed on to me was the ability to get after kids that messed up, call them names, make fun of them, and yet still have them and their parents love me when the day is done. I routinely tell parents, "I am no different than Dan Brody except that my pitch isn't as high as his." I would look at some of our boys and call them stupid, I would call them ugly, I would tell them that I would trade them for a corndog in a heartbeat and they STILL loved me. Granted they knew I was joking but you have to admit that's still a gift. When a mother once came to me and asked me why her son didn't start I told her, "Because he wasn't good enough." She laughed and said ok and then walked away. Thanks Dad.

Chapter 3

Favorite Players

Jay-Michael and Jordan Kinney

My Life at The Mitch: A Little League Baseball Story

As a little league coach you are expected to teach the fundamentals of the game to young kids and impart on them life lessons whenever the opportunity arises. During the baseball season for the C-K Braves there is rarely a day off. This means that I spend roughly 2 1/2 hours a day, for three months, with other people's children. Usually about a third of the way through the season I am trying to talk Mick into giving the kids a day off. I put it in the context of "They deserve a reward." Whenever the Braves get beat the other coach usually gets drenched with a Gatorade cooler. That's how often my team loses. So I tell Mick that the kids haven't lost a game and they deserve a day off. What that really means is, I'm getting sick of being around these kids every stinking day and I need a break or else I'm going to choke someone.

Any little league coach worth his salt will tell you that he loves all his kids and wants to teach them all equally. Then every so often you will come by a little league coach like me that is an honest coach. I will tell you that there are some kids that I absolutely love coaching and being around and then there are the select few that I have coached over the years that make me want to sneak off somewhere and beat my head off a wall until unconsciousness is reached. I've always found it best to unleash beatings on myself instead of taking it out on 9-12 year old boys. After all, they can't help it. They are just little kids. I've been fortunate in the fact that those types of kids have come few and far between. Make no mistake though, there have been a few. There have been times that I have stepped off to the side and said half heartedly, "You know Mick, I really hate that kid. Do you think I would get in trouble if I just punch him in the nose?" I would wishfully ask, "How old is he Mick, 12?" "No Matt, he's 10." Mick would reply with a grin. #@$@#@# ! Two more years!!

Jake Adams was my first favorite player that I had in my coaching career.

Matthew Cisco

As I said before, the mere fact that he bathed in the joy of driving Dan crazy made me love him even more. At that point in my second year Dan was starting to wear thin on me and any misery that Jake put him through was bliss that we both enjoyed. After my dad passed and Dan greeted me with a hug I haven't harbored an ill thought towards him since. It went from my enjoying his misery out of pure meanness to me enjoying his misery just out of harmless fun. After I saw the true side of Dan Brody I wouldn't take delight in his suffering anymore. However, I was able to step back, since I wasn't directly involved, and enjoyed Jake's antics for their pure comedic value. Dan just happened to be the punch line in the majority of Jake's stunts.

Jake Kinney- The all-time worst 9 year old in the history of Mitch Stadium

My Life at The Mitch: A Little League Baseball Story

In my third year with the team we drafted a nine year old boy named Jake Kinney. He had a younger brother named Jordan that made Jake's pick more understandable. Even at Jordan's young age you could see that he would be a pretty good ballplayer so we picked up his brother to make Jordan an automatic pick. Jake Kinney played the same time as Jake Adams so to make things easy we referred to Adams as "Big Jake" and Kinney as "Little Jake." As the preseason practices wore on "Little Jake" was moved from place to place. Mostly though, his time was spent in right field. Right field, as you know, is the place where all coaches try to hide the weakest of their starters. Needless to say, Jake Kinney was a third string right fielder at best. I would talk to Mick from time to time about the progress of some of the players on our team. "Little Jake's" name would eventually come up and I was never able to form the words to describe the level of talent that he showed off. Mick, Dan, and I would hold a coaches meeting prior to opening day for us to decide where we were going to play the kids. We all agreed that "Little Jakes" time would be spent in right field. At that time it finally hit me on how to best describe Jake Kinney. He was, without a doubt, the worst little league baseball player in the all-time history of little league baseball. Jake Kinney's role in preseason was to take up a spot that could've better been filled by a blind boy with two broken arms.

Opening Day came and Jake Kinney took his rightful place by the water cooler in the dugout. As any coach can tell you and Dan Brody can attest to, the dugout can be a hectic place full of little boys with loads of energy. They are more interested in spitting seeds into a cup, drinking water and spitting it out between their teeth. They would much rather look for mommy and get some gum to chew on. Every inning at least one kid had to go to the bathroom or lean out the dugout to get snacks from mom, except for one. A beautiful surprise was about to occur. When our kids were in the field they had a play with a runner on second base and one man out. A ground ball was hit to our shortstop and he threw on to first and got the out while the runner at second advanced to third. Among the spitting seeds, bubblegum bubbles popping and water be poured on people Jake Kinney looked at me and asked, "Matt, if I were at shortstop and that play happened should I check the runner before throwing to first?" At first I thought to myself, "Yea right, like YOU'LL ever be at short." Then it hit me. This boy wasn't spitting seeds or dumping water on people. Amid all the chaos this nine year old boy was watching the game. As his nine year old year wore on the questions kept coming. Jake was getting smarter and learning the game but since he had no talent at all it didn't really matter. By this time I was so comfortable with him I went to his mother and said with all honesty, "Vikki, your boy is the worst little league player ever to enter this league. I just thought you should know that because I wouldn't trade him for the best player in the state." Throughout his time with us Jake kept asking questions and working his butt off in practice and then a funny thing happened. By the time he was 12 years old he had made himself into a pretty good ballplayer. He turned himself into a pretty good fielder and a reliable hitter and made himself a starter. There has never been a kid that I was more proud of than Jake Kinney. I knew that anything good he did on the baseball field was a direct result of the hard work and effort he put into practice. Mick, Dan or I could take no credit for it.

 This was a young boy that was eager to learn and way more than willing to put the time in to make himself a better player. There is no doubt in my mind that had he been blessed with natural ability and that be combined with his willingness to improve the sky would've been the limit for him. As Jake's time with our team came to a close he moved on to Babe Ruth ball. Jordan was now on our team and Jake would come to watch him play after his own game was over. He would always seem to make a beeline to me so he could tell me about the hit's he got or the plays he made in the field.

My Life at The Mitch: A Little League Baseball Story

It's as if he was telling me this in the hopes that I would be proud of him. My one and only regret in little league is that I never really illustrated to him how proud I was of him. Granted, if he got a hit for us or made a play in the field I would congratulate him just like I did everyone else. Jake, though, was an exception. If you think that I am taking shots at a young boy then that is because you're not understanding me. I point out that he was the worst 9 year old of all time and he was. I have no trouble saying that because of what he turned himself into. Will Jake Kinney go pro? No. Jake Kinney now plays high school ball. He plays high school ball because of the work he put into it and the millions of questions that he asked me over a four year period. Kid's in little league are taught by their coaches. Few if any little league players ask questions and just follow the orders of what they've been told. Jake followed the orders as best he could but also wanted to know why he was doing it. Ahhh, if only all ballplayers could be that way. Jakes leaving little league was also a passing of sorts. It was around this time that our team, the Cubs, was disbanded and we became the Braves.

 With both Jake's now off the team our dugout lacked a character. We still had boy's on our team that were funny and had good times but none that really filled that role left by the two Jakes. Try outs were about to begin for the new year and "The Commish" Paul Billups informed all the coaches that there would be no twelve year olds or eleven year olds that wouldn't make a team. He wanted to make sure that all the older kids that were trying out be picked so they could enjoy the little league experience for at least two years.

 As I stated earlier, tryouts can be a nerve racking time for a young kid. Kids are sent out onto a baseball field all by themselves with all the coaches in the league sitting in the bleachers with notebooks in their laps ready to grade them. In my years of coaching I have seen other coaches

36

with detailed charts to grade players and even laptop computers to store all their information on. I look at other coaches as a grown man and think how silly it is, I can only imagine the added nervousness it must add to a young boy or girl to see this. The kids are tried out in order of their age. First there are the nine year olds and so on. It always seems that the best of each group go first. I watch these can't miss kid's tryout and can't help but wonder what the other kids of lesser talent are thinking and how nervous they must be. Each year at tryouts I always find myself back in 1981 and I feel bad for the present day kids that must be feeling what I felt.

So as each kid tried out I would talk with Mick who had his notebook in hand. He would have each kids name wrote down and next to it have columns that rated throwing, running, fielding and hitting. Scoring would be rated from 1 being the worst to 5 being the best. My system is this. Yes or No. I will write yes by a kids name if I want him or no if I don't. Usually this is done on Mick's pages. This always seemed to irk him because I had defaced the beautiful scoring system that he has created on the pages of his notebook.

When we got to the eleven year old group there was one kid that stood out to me. He was the worst player in that age group. He was probably about 5'10 and weighed close to 200 pounds if not more. He had an absolute rocket for an arm but couldn't hit the backstop if he tried. He dropped most of the balls that were thrown to him and he didn't cleanly field one ground ball. My heart was breaking for this kid. Then on his final ground ball that was hit to him he bobbled it. He then bent over to pick it up and almost fell over. He grabbed the ball only to drop it again. During this most traumatic time in his life this kid was laughing. It was a genuine laugh too and not one out of nervousness. He picked up the ball and threw it 100 mph towards the coach on the field and about 20 feet to the left of him. When it came time for him to bat he would swing with all his might and miss the ball by three feet easy. After each time he swung the bat he would have to step out of the box and pull his pants back up. This kid was

37

laughing the entire time he was out there and absolutely enjoying every minute of it despite his only talent being a rocket arm he couldn't control. I grabbed Mick's book at wrote next to his name Y.E.S.! The boys name, Trevor Newton.

I pestered Mick about him the entire tryout and told him that I HAD to have that boy on my team. When draft night came I was actually nervous about this kid going to a team that wouldn't reveal his full talents. Our team needed another "Jake Adams" and this kid fit that role perfectly. We had two draft picks left. By this time all the top players were long removed from the board and people started picking up the 11 and 12 year olds that Paul demanded be taken. I figured that it was a high probability that someone would use their last pick on Trevor. There were still kids on the board that had some talent in the next to last round and I felt the other coaches would go after them. Still I hadn't convinced myself that someone wouldn't snag him earlier. Our turn had come up. Mick and Dan were going over their lists and I kept quietly chanting, "Trevor, Trevor, Trevor." Mick decided to make me happy and give me the player that I most coveted in the draft. I landed Trevor Newton, he was now a C-K Brave.

Trevor spent his eleven year old year fulfilling the role that I drafted him for. Kid's in little league tend to go through mood swings for whatever reason. Not Trevor. He was always laughing, always trying to cheer other people up. I took him under my wing and made no bones about it on the team that I adored Trevor Newton. The other kids on the team really took to him as well. My son Jay-Michael, Jordan Kinney, Bryer Brewer all took to "Big Trev". I really liked that because a kid his size is usually the subject of ridicule and being made fun of by other kids his age. So naturally, Trevor took his place in right field when it came to his turn to play. He really didn't do much that I can recall his eleven year old year besides making it a joy to come to every game. His laugh was the type that made you laugh as soon as you heard it.

38

Then came Trevor's twelve year old year. After getting a year under his belt Trevor was actually showing signs of improvement. He was starting to catch fly balls and getting hits every so often. My son and his buddies would always walk to a place after school that they called "The Bamboo Forest." Jay-Michael brought home this stick made of bamboo that was about the length of a 28" baseball bat. I kept it in my car for the longest time. The year was movingly along as planned. We were running away with yet another league title but as far as Trevor was concerned nothing really had changed. His heart of gold provided another fond memory. Jay-Michael had made a sensational diving play at shortstop for the 3rd out. The stands all went crazy. I was a proud Papa. As my son picked himself up off the ground I saw this huge red haired boy sprinting on a beeline from right field straight for him. Like picking up an empty sack of potato's Trevor flung Jay-Michael into the air and carried him off the field in a bear hug that had me slightly concerned about him for a fleeting period of time.

Trevor had been destroying the baseball in batting practice but was unable to carry that over into the game. He was also catching pop-ups with regularity so we moved him to left field. For whatever reason I had the bright idea to tell Trevor that if he ever hit a homerun in a game I would let him whip me with the bamboo stick I had after the ballgame. Why this came to my mind as an incentive for Trevor I will never know. The season was winding down. Trevor had provided me and the boys on the team with almost 2 years of laughter each and every day. Then the day came that Trevor hit his peak. In the last at bat of the day for Trevor he slowly lumbered his big frame into the right handed batter's box and took his place. I hollered at "Big Trev" to swing with everything he had. The first pitch came right down the middle and with Ruthian like majesty Trevor swung the bat. He missed it by about 2 feet. If Trevor didn't hit a ball on his first swing you could see that he would get down on himself. I yelled at Trevor, "Great swing Trev. Do it again!" The pitch came, PING, the ball soared almost a mile into the air. When I first saw it leave his bat I went

39

My Life at The Mitch: A Little League Baseball Story

back in time to my twelve year old year in all-stars when I was robbed of a homerun. That thought left my mind when I saw that this ball wasn't coming down and I was comforted by the fact that the outfield fence at "The Mitch" is about 7 feet high and no little leaguer was going to rob it. The crowd went absolutely crazy. By this time the parents and other coaches had all grown to love Trevor. He rounded first base and missed the bag. I hollered at him to come back and touch it which he did. He rounded the bases in his homerun trot with a smile on his face that he had earned over a course of two years. I couldn't have been happier for him and the thought that I was going to be caned by him after the game didn't cross my mind until he reached home plate. He looked at me and slightly bent over and smacked his butt signaling to me what I was in for.

After the game all the kids were hollering for me to go to my car and get the bamboo stick. I'm a man of my word so I did. Now before I tell you what all unfolded I need to stress to you again the strength and power that resided in the body of this twelve year old boy. Trevor and I walked to the pitcher's mound so all the kids and parents could see what was going on. Trevor was happier about it than I was. I must admit I was a little bit nervous about what I had gotten myself into. Trevor gripped the bamboo stick and steadied himself as if he were ready to go deep one more time that day. I bent over and closed my eyes. THWACK!!! The pain was so intense that I almost vomited all over the pitcher's mound. My butt was bruised for the next two weeks and about a week went by before I was able to sit down without feeling pain. As I was walking off the field with my arm over "Big Trev's" shoulder he looked at me and said, "I didn't want to do it at first Matt. I didn't want to hurt you. So instead, I swung the stick left handed." A boy with a heart of gold and strength yet undiscovered. I shudder at the thought of what my reaction would've been had he swung right handed.

Later in the year, after we had wrapped up another league title we let Trevor start a game for us on the mound. Dan is a student of the game

40

and respects the game too much for any Brave to make a mockery of it. So we decided that as soon as Trevor got into trouble we would take him out. We were playing the Dodgers that day. On their team was the best player in the league Anthony Evans. He lead off the game as "Big Trev" toed the rubber. You have to understand that Anthony could hit a dime if you threw it towards the plate. The kid could hit anything and anyone. I think it's safe to say that he got on base at least 95% of the time. And when he got on base you might as well go ahead and put a run on the board because he was going to score. I had never been more nervous for a kid that wasn't my own. Trevor looked in and got the signal. Why he was looking for a signal I don't know because all he had was a fast ball. He rocked into his stance and unleashed his cannon. ZIP! Strike one! Evans had swung completely through the ball. It's the first time I saw him overmatched. The crowd was cheering as if we were in Williamsport. Trevor stepped back on the rubber and again got the sign for some reason. "Big Trev" unleashes the cannon, ZIP, strike two!!! Anthony had swung about 2 seconds late as the catcher's mitt caught the ball and it sounded like a bomb had went off. What was I witnessing? The crowd is going mad, Trevor has pinpoint control, Anthony Evans is about to strike out for the first time all year long. What a way for this kid to start the game. Well, this wasn't a movie and the next 12 pitches all hit about halfway up the backstop. The bases were loaded, all on walks, with nobody out. It was time to pull Trevor from the game. I hated the walk I had to take towards the mound. All he wanted to do was pitch and I had to take that away from him. Pity applause was coming from the stands and my heart was aching for him. I reached the mound and there was the smile. "It kind of got away from me didn't it Matt?" Trevor said. When 90% of little league pitchers would end up crying at such a performance here was Trevor, smiling. Just like that kid two years earlier that couldn't field a ground ball. Trevor Newton, one of my all time favorites.

Chapter 4

Umpires

Me umpiring during the 2006 Tournament of Champions

Matthew Cisco

You can't play the game without them. In our league at C-K there is an umpiring schedule for all the coaches. The coaches themselves have to umpire the games that are given to them or at least get them covered. More often than not the coaches will get the games covered by the same one or two volunteers that are around the league during that year that are not coaches. These young guys are eager to get out there and do some top notch umpiring. Some do it because they just actually love to umpire. Other's do it because they see little league baseball at "The Mitch" as their personal stepping stone to the major leagues. What these poor young souls don't realize is that they are perfecting their craft in games where the final score will inevitably be 24 to 22. I guess that's why it usually isn't the same volunteers that we see at the field with each passing year. Who knows, maybe they got called up to the show or maybe they realized umpiring for free or for the occasional corn dog wasn't all it was cracked up to be. Needless to say, you can't play the game without umpires.

When I first started coaching I would umpire any game that Mick asked me to. Home plate or first base is where I wanted to be. When you are behind the plate you have to make a call with every pitch and at first base you will occasionally get the bang bang play where you really have to sell your call. Every so often I would pay tribute to my father with his Kenova-wide famous Blues Brother's safe call. I would   umpire games that the Braves didn't even have scheduled for them just telling the other coaches to go on home.

However, I learned quickly to find out what teams were playing when I had to call a game behind the plate. Do you remember those huge foam chest protectors that the umpires used to wear back in the 70's? Little League baseball should really consider bringing those back. My point being is most little leagues are equipped with subpar umpire equipment and let's face it, little "Johnny" behind the plate isn't exactly Johnny Bench. There were some games that I looked forward to calling behind the plate because I knew they would be well played games and low scoring. More importantly, I knew the catcher would be able to catch the ball. This meant, no bruises, no pain. The games I dreaded were games when big Billy Evans, an out of control left hander who threw upwards of 115 mph was pitching to a catcher that was no taller once he got up from his crouch. I would tell these kids before the game, "Catch, you don't let the ball hit me one time and I will buy you cheese sticks after the game." Unfortunately, I was never able to make good on that offer.

Most home plate umpires get in the traditional squat stance. Some pick the outside corner to set up on and some pick the inside corner to set up on. I used to be that way as well but after taking about 30 balls off the shoulder, about 100 balls off the inside of my thigh and the occasional high fastball to the facemask I developed a new strategy. I squat where the catcher squat. Little Johnny behind home plate was 3 feet tall when he squat, I made myself 3 feet tall when I squat. No more inside or outside corner. Where the catcher went I went. I made myself tall enough so when the pitcher threw the ball my face was almost resting on the catchers shoulder.

Doing league games during the regular season was always fun for me. I made all the calls as best I could missing only maybe one or two strike calls a year. If you ask me I have never blown a call at first base. However, I know of one coach that would disagree with me. One night I was calling a game between the Cardinals and the Pirates and I was scheduled for first base. I was looking forward to this game because it was against two evenly matched teams. If I recall correctly the score was 5 to 4 in favor of the Cardinals. In the bottom of the sixth inning the Pirates had one out with a runner on second base. Cody Duvall, one of their better players on the team stepped into the batter's box. The first pitch came and Cody smashed the ball to deep right center field and hit the base of the wall.

44

Matthew Cisco

Cody was an excellent ballplayer. The kid could hit and could run like the wind. Once I saw the ball was uncatchable, as any good umpire would do, I turned to first base to watch the runner hit the bag. Cody rounded first and headed for second. Barry Meade, the first base coach for the Pirates screamed, "He touched it, he touched it, he touched it!" What I saw plain as day was Cody missing the inside of the bag by about an inch. Cody slid into home safely. Pirates win! Pirates win! The stands are going crazy. The coach for the Cardinals, Mark Duty, motioned for his kids to stay on the field. He then instructed his pitcher on how to properly appeal to first base. Barry Meade hadn't moved from his spot in the coach's box. I think he knew what was coming. Once I saw Cody rounding first base I knew he would score. When I saw him miss the bag I thought to myself, "Damn it Cody, you've put me in a tough spot here." Part of me was hoping that Mark didn't notice Cody missing the bag and I could just go on home without any headache. Truthfully, I don't think Mark noticed it at all but he heard Barry yelling that he touched it so he figured he would give it a shot. What am I to do? Do I take a thrilling walk off inside the park homerun away from a little boy or do I uphold the rule of the game. I know Mark Duty. If I give a safe call on the appeal, that would be the end of it. Mark was the kind of coach that could care less if his team ever won a game. He was truly there for the kids. The only lesson he wanted to impart on them during their two hours at the ball field was play hard and have fun. Unlike the Braves dugout where you heard occasional buckets flying and scorebooks being slammed you always heard nothing but laughs coming out of the Cardinals dugout. I knew if I were to make the proper call then the stands would be in an uproar. I underestimated the reaction. The Cardinal pitcher stepped off the rubber and threw to the first baseman who stepped on the bag. Whatever I was going to call I knew I would have to sell it as best I could. "Boom", I screamed as I threw my fist forward. I called him out. No sooner did I get finished with my motion Barry Meade was right in front of me as I stood tall. "He missed the bag Barry", I said.

My Life at The Mitch: A Little League Baseball Story

Barry yelled, "You blew that call Matthew! He touched it! He touched it!" Just as I was getting ready to toss Barry I thought that maybe I should just turn around and walk away from him. So I did. As soon as I turned away there was Jeff Baldwin, the other Pirates coach, who had sprinted from the dugout on the third base side to argue my call. "How can you call that", asked Jeff. I simply said, "Easy Jeff, he missed the bag." After about two minutes more of arguing everyone went their separate ways when they realized I wasn't changing my mind. While I was being tag teamed by two coaches at first base I took a brief second to gaze into the Cardinals dugout. What I saw was Mark Duty having himself quite the chuckle at my expense. For Duty there was never a situation that didn't call for a laugh. After the game "The Commish", Paul Billups, told me to never allow that to happen again and toss any coach that comes at me that way. He never mentioned what a good call I made. He was more disappointed in me for what I allowed to happen afterwards.

I don't want to give the impression that Barry Meade and Jeff Baldwin are bad people or bad coaches. They are both good people that I like very much. That one night though the heat of the moment got to them. As for Mark Duty, from that point forward whenever I called a game behind the plate when his team played he would complain about every, and I mean EVERY, ball call that I gave to his pitcher. I knew he was doing it as a joke though, but give Mark credit, he knew my routine when I was behind the plate. If you complain and I don't like the way you are doing it I will give you a quick glance with my mask still on. If you continue to complain and I don't approve of the manner in which it's done I will give you a quick glance with my mask off. After that if you complain then the mask will come off and you will get tossed. Nevertheless, Mark never ended up getting tossed from a game and would retire from coaching at "The Mitch" a few years later. He was one of those characters of the game that my dad would always talk about. Umpiring has gotten a little dull at "The Mitch" ever since he left. Now the only excitement I get when umpiring behind the plate is the occasional "OH MY" or "GOOD NIGHT" I get from Scott Milum when he disagrees with a ball/strike call that I make.

The reason I always enjoyed doing regular season games was because all the coaches knew me. My "flaw" if you want to call it one is giving kids credit for when they make great plays. If a kid makes a diving catch for an out I may give him a pat on the back when he goes to the dugout or if a pitcher strikes out the side I may give him a handshake as he passes by. If I were to do such a thing during all-star play the parents, coaches, and "top umpires" of our district would have a fit. Why not congratulate a kid? If grown adults takes this gesture as me cheating for the other team or being biased for one person or another then too bad. It's amazing how much more fun these kids would have if we were to sometimes remove the adult equation from the game.

My three biggest influences in umpiring were my dad, Paul Billups and Durwood Merrill. After my second year of umpiring Paul gave me a book by Durwood Merrill titled "You're Out and You're Ugly Too". Durwood Merrill was an American League umpire in the 70's, 80's, and 90's. I highly recommend this book for any young, aspiring umpire. As I read through the pages it validated everything that was ever taught to me by my father. Reggie Jackson was quoted in the book as referring to Durwood as the "Reggie Jackson of umpiring." I came to learn that Merrill took his job but not himself seriously. He knew how to interact with the players and coaches. There is even a picture of him leaning up against a wall, in between innings, and talking with the fans. This would be a major no-no in my district. An umpire with a personality? Unheard of! Like my father, Merrill realized that there WAS a place in the game for characteristic umpires so long as they themselves didn't try to be the show. Fortunately for me Paul has never asked for the book back. I always seem to dust it off

My Life at The Mitch: A Little League Baseball Story

at the start of each new season and always seem to find a story that I can relate to from the season gone by.

After a few years of umpiring Paul felt I was ready to get my feet wet with some all-star games. It was during this time that Paul really started taking me under his wing. I did some city tournament games and some all-star games and Paul would always be there with advice on what he felt I did wrong or what I did right. The following year Paul asked if I would like to go to Elkins, West Virginia with him and call some of the games in the West Virginia state tournament and even offered to pay my way. Those were the only games that I ever got to umpire with him and a great learning experience for me as well. After we did our one or two games a day we would have nothing left to do all day long so he drove me to places like Senica Rock and Blackwater Falls. It was during these little outings that I learned that Paul had umpired games with my dad many years ago. Hearing him share those stories kind of made me feel a little closer to dad and each time I took the field after that I kind of felt him out there with me. From that point forward Paul was the only person I would ever accept criticism from as far as my umpiring goes. If Paul would say Matthew you need to do "X" in this situation and "Y" in this situation I would take to heart what he said and apply it. If the "top umpires" in our district were to ever give me an opinion I would just let it fall on deaf ears.

The following year Paul was able to secure the State Tournament of Champions. Little League baseball allowed for 9-10 year old All-Stars to compete beyond the state level for the first time ever and Paul was able to get it held in our town. He told me he wanted me to umpire and scheduled me for 4 games. The toughest one I had was the game in which I had the plate between Kentucky and Virginia. It was a closely contested game that could've gone either way. By the third inning I had told all three coaches from Virginia that if I heard another complaint out of them made towards

48

any umpire I was going to toss them. Our talk seemed to quiet them for the rest of the game. They were behind so naturally they felt it was the umpires fault. Well their team came back to take the lead so naturally they felt we were doing a good job. Now it was time for Kentucky to take its shot. I didn't really have trouble with the coaches. Any complaints they had they handled it the proper way by lowering their heads when they walked by to voice their complaints. Any good umpire should let stuff like that slide because they are going out of their way not to show you up. Kentucky's arguing came from their fans. The majority of their fans were along the leftfield wall at Mitch Stadium. All umpires should learn to block out what they hear from the stands or at least ignore it. "You're terrible!" "You can't see anything blue!" "You blew that call ump!" All of these things I find acceptable even when they are yelled at me in a murderous tone. However, if you use foul language against an umpire at a game played by children then your rights will be revoked and you will be sent home. The first three innings the Kentucky fans were the picture perfect fans, they were ahead. The last three innings was the complete opposite. After two innings of hearing, this large section of fans down the left field line, refer to myself and my crew as "Cheaters" my patience began to wear thin. Some may think I overact when being called a cheater. Nothing makes me madder than idiot parents who actually think I would cheat any kid, on any team, from any state out of anything. After I heard the first curse word I let it go. When they began to use curse words as adjectives I called for time. I calmly walked from behind the plate without a clue of what I was going to do. I stood behind the third base bag, removed my mask and informed the entire section that if I heard any more bad language or the word "cheater" being directed at any of my umpires I would clear out the whole section and send them home. Virginia won the game and after it was over I saw a group of about 10 Kentucky parents waiting for me outside of the press box. God bless Paul Billups. He wanted to call the police and get me an escort. I told him there was no need and I walked outside. All at once, here they all came up to me. "We're sorry", they said. "Please don't think that all of us are that way. Thank you for shutting them up. We have listened to them the entire year and nobody has ever said anything to them." This was said to me by parents from Kentucky just mere moments after the "top umpires" in my district suggested that I use more restraint. I realized that my all-star days were numbered after that. All-star play is too high tense for me. Not because of the high level of play but because of the number of parents and coaches that think they will be invited to the White House to meet the President if they win this tournament.

I did one more Tournament of Champions after that and decided to hang it up. The irony was, not because of the parents or the coaches, but because of the umpires. They were all robots. Just like the ones you see doing Little League World Series games. I find no problem with trying to look and act professional but it shouldn't be because you think you ARE professional. It should be just for the pageantry of the event. There were no "characters" anymore. You know the type of robot umpires I'm talking about or maybe I'm the only one. The ones that stare at a base for 5 seconds after they have called a runner out. The ones that sprint halfway into the outfield and stand in between innings. FYI, you are LITTLE LEAGUE umpires, take the corncob out and relax. I'm talking about the kind of robot umpires that have the same text book mechanics behind the plate for every call of the game. When I did my last Tournament of Champions I refused to run out to the outfield and stand like I was a major league umpire. You know what I did instead? I talked with the kids. I asked if they liked the field and if they were enjoying their stay. I talked with the coaches and asked them the same. I could tell that this irked the other robot umpires I was with. Some of them local and some that had traveled to give their time. I'm not saying their way of doing things is bad. It's just not my cup of tea. I felt all hope was lost and I had already told Paul I was finished. I got to sit and enjoy the last game of the evening from the stands. There was a father and son combination doing first and second base for that game. They had traveled down from Indiana to volunteer their time to umpire some of the games. I had talked with them a time or two throughout the tournament and they both seemed like pleasant people. In between the bottom half of the first inning there they went halfway into the outfield. "Oh no", I thought "They've turned them into robot's too." I was just about to leave when over the P.A. came the Macarena song. You know the one I'm talking about. It's the song with the goofy dance and "Eeeeeeeeeh Macarena" is the only thing you can understand. I gazed in wonderment out towards right centerfield and there stood father and son from Indiana doing the Macarena in front of a packed house without a care in the world while the other stoic, robot umpires looked on. I later overheard some of them talking about these two gentlemen as if they were somehow an embarrassment. What fun it would be if all were like the two gentlemen from Indiana.

Chapter 5

Parents

Proud Mom and Dad with Jay-Michael in Princeton, WV during the the 2007 WV State Baseball Tournament.

Parents are the lifeblood of little league baseball. Because of the parents you have coaches. Because of the parents you have people that run the concession stand. Because of the parents you have someone to keep the scorebook and run the scoreboard. Because of the parents you also have the occasional bursts of rage that can send chaos running through the bleachers and dugouts. Every league has at least one or two parents that people just dread to be around. These are the parents that think their little boy is on the verge of signing a contract with a big league team. These are the parents that think if little Johnny took a pitch then it MUST HAVE been a ball and the umpiring is cheating their son out of future greatness. These are the parents that think if little Johnny gets taken out of a game then the coaches must hate him and be a part of the conspiracy to keep their boy down. These are the parents that nobody wants to sit by at ball games. These are the parents that put unbelievable pressure on the shoulders of little children playing a child's game. These are the parents that will verbally abuse their kid for making an error, the same kid they claim to love. I sometimes wonder if their fat behind's could've made the play. I wonder if they ever even played the game before at all. If you don't know any parents like this in your league then chances are YOU are the parents that I am talking about.

In all my years of coaching little league baseball I have been truly blessed with fantastic parents on my team. I'm not sure if all our parents just agreed with what Mick, Dan and I were doing or if they were all the ideal little league parent that each coach dreams about. As a coach I feel that if you show a genuine interest in a child and are fair with them then you usually shouldn't have any problems out of the parents. I can only think of one example in which I had to deal with an outburst from one of our parents on the team.

Let me set the stage for you. My first two years of coaching when it came time to drafting players it was done on a bidding system. Each team was allotted 10,000 points a year and whatever they didn't spend they were allowed to be carried over to the following year's draft. This particular year we were about middle of the pack as far as points were concerned. There were two boys that I had my eyes on but I feared we wouldn't have enough points to draft either one let alone both of them. The boy's names were Tyler Edwards and T.L. Bryant. In my estimation these two boys were in the top three of the entire draft. The top players in the draft usually went for around 8,000-9,500 points so you can understand why I was a little concerned knowing we only had about 12,000 points out our disposal and having to pick up four players. We held the draft in an office room at Mick's place of work on a Monday evening. As we all sat around snacking on a food spread we all talked about the players in the coming draft. That's when I put the plan in motion. I dropped a little rumor in the room that the parents of Tyler and T.L. were both nuts. I would tell people that I knew both of the dad's, which in reality I only knew Tyler's dad Carl, and that both of them were a pain to deal with. I let it "slip" that they constantly argued with coaches and always tried to take over teams that their boy's were on. Long story short, we got Tyler Edwards for 2,500 and T.L. Bryant for 1,700 points. In the four years that Tyler was on my team I never heard one complaint from his dad. He never second guessed any of us, never showed himself at games or practices and even helped us when we needed him to. He was the ideal parent. Tyler Edwards was a STEAL and to this day I don't lose a wink of sleep over it.

In the four years that T.L. was on the team the only complaint that I got from his dad Tom or his mom Jennifer was that I was too easy on him. Can you believe that? A parent gets on me for being too easy? I was living the dream baby. There are a few things you need to understand about Tom Bryant. First picture Paul Bunyon. Ok, now you know what he looks like. Secondly, he was a good man that would help whenever we needed. Tom also played a role in the renovation of Mitch Stadium. Third and

54

finally, when Tom became upset about something it was like a tidal wave slowly building and you wanted to be nowhere near the coast when it crashed. I can count on one hand the amount of times I saw Tom Bryant upset at a little league game in the 4 years I coached his son. Three of those times his anger was directed at his own boy but since parents aren't allowed on the field or in the dugouts I was able to defuse the situation. Then there was the one and only incident I have ever had to deal with Tom Bryant. I know what you are thinking. I said that the only complaint I got from Tom or Jennifer was that I was too easy on T.L. Well, this wrath was aimed at Mick. I just happened to play the role of hero that saved the day. It could've been ugly. I have no problem with saying that Tom could've squeezed the life out of me if he wanted to.

T.L. was having a bad game in the field and at the plate. As I recall I think he booted a couple of balls and was just having an all around bad game. Mick decided that for that day he would pull T.L. from the game and sit him on the bench. Keep in mind I didn't actually see what method Mick used to remove T.L. and I didn't hear what exactly he said to him either. The only thing I heard was the curdling scream, "Miiiiiiiiiiiiiiiiiiick!" coming from some Paul Bunyon looking guy standing behind the dugout. As the inning came to an end I noticed that Mick had taken an unusual place to stand way over in the corner of the dugout away from where the players go in and out. It was a nice secluded little spot that I have never seen Mick stand in. I'm sure it was just a coincidence. Needless to say I met King Kong at the field entrance door beside the first base dugout. He stood about 9' 4, his arms swelled like Popeye's and his face was redder than Rudolph's shiny nose. I stood there talking to him face to face trying to be the voice of reason. To this day I don't know what Tom said to me. I don't think Tom's knows either. He was speaking in some weird little league baseball tongue that I had never heard before. Needless to say the crisis was avoided. Whatever venom it was that Tom was spewing he felt 100% relief after he got it out of his system. Tom and Jennifer Bryant were great little league parents to have on our team.

Melinda Adams is the ideal little league parent. She is the mother of the infamous "Big Jake" Adams. Mick, Dan, and I have coached three of her four boys. Jake, Seth, and Caleb all three shared the last name of Adams and all three were as different as night and day. All were a joy to coach. Like I said before though, none could make me laugh more than "Big Jake." Melinda has also been the treasurer at Mitch Stadium for as long as I can remember. If you ask me she is the female version of the field's namesake. Each year after the season was over she and her husband Chuck would allow our entire team of boys, their parents, and the occasional kid that wasn't even on the team to hold a pool party at their house. If you can imagine a standard in ground swimming pool in a backyard being filled by at least fifteen screaming kids and the occasional wet dog trying to get a tennis ball you can understand what an undertaking this is. No expense was spared by them. Being the organizer, Melinda would always make sure everything was set up and Chuck would be sweating away on the grill making food for twenty-five or more people. One year at the party I was fortunate enough to beat Melinda at her own game. The game was ping pong. She has yet to pay up on the wager we made. At the end of each party we have the award ceremonies when we say goodbye to the outgoing twelve year olds on our team and the parents always seem to chip in and get gifts for Mick, Dan and I. The year my dad passed away I was fortunate enough to have everyone in one room and thank again the children and their parents for the support they showed for me at dad's funeral. Melinda allowing our kids to invade her home at the end of the year is what made that moment possible for me. It has to be more than dedication to her kids. All three of her boys that we have coached have already played their time in little league and she is still there. So I'm really not sure if it's tireless dedication to C-K Little League Baseball year in and year out or if its people that just take for granted that

56

she is there and just assume she will be there when needed. She still allows us to raid her home at the end of each year without a kid of her own being on the team. She is the ultimate "team mom" even long after her son's took their last swing at "The Mitch." Every little league organization would be better off if they had a "Melinda Adams" volunteering her time. We are truly fortunate to have her at Mitch Stadium.

My all-time favorite parent whose son I have coached is my son's mother. This may seem biased to you all but you have to meet this woman. Granted, she didn't put the time in at the field that Melinda did but the time she spent there she put to use better than anyone I have ever seen. Her name is Melissa Brubeck. You may notice that her last name is different than mine and that is because she is my ex-wife but also my best friend. She remarried after we divorced and went on to have two more children Karli and Mason. Karli is the apple of my eye. I love her dearly. Mason of course is Jay-Michael's brother and in little league terms makes him an automatic. This also makes him a steal! My son's last year of little league was Mason's first year. It was good that the two brothers got to play at least one year together and it provided myself with my favorite year of coaching little league to date. Mason's dad Justin also helped us out in practice from time to time and would sit in the dugout whenever Mick, Dan or I couldn't make it to a game. At each and every game was Melissa sitting in the stands. She wasn't your normal mom that spent 70% of the time cheering on the boys and the other 30% catching up on the Mitch Stadium rumor mill. Don't get me wrong. I loved all of our mom's. I'm just dubbing Melissa as my favorite. Melissa is a school teacher. This in itself takes a special person to do. She has the gifted ability to pick up on a child's strengths and weakness. She can tell what makes a child happy and she can sense what makes a child feel vulnerable. All kids deserve to share in the feeling of listening to people cheer and applaud them. It gives them a sense of superstardom no matter how fleeting. Unfortunately I

57

My Life at The Mitch: A Little League Baseball Story

have coached kid's who's mom's I have never seen. I have coached kid's who's dad's I can count on one hand the times they have shown up to watch them play over a four year period. We have coached boys whose mother, father, grandfather, grandmother, aunt or uncle I have never seen. These are the kids that walk or ride their bikes to the field. I try to treat all my boys on the team equally regardless of their situation with the exception of Trevor Newton of course. When the kids, whose mom or dad would never show, would step up to the plate Melissa would cheer louder for them than she did her own. When they struck out she would yell, "That's ok 'Tommy', GREAT TRY!" When those kids would get a hit or make a nice play in the field, she would go absolutely nuts. You have to understand how loud this woman can be. I've seen the local police at games before and I often wonder if people that live in the houses near the field have called in noise complaints when Melissa starts cheering. The only time you see the dark side of her is if she feels you have wronged one of her babies. I will explain more about that later on.

When Melissa cheers for our boy's on the team there isn't one of them that doesn't end up not smiling. Naturally, after they get a hit they will smile but when they hear and see her, the smile grows even wider and for a fleeting moment it's as if they can see the Hall of Fame on the horizon. The awesome thing about our mom's on the team is that they will all cheer a little harder for the boy's without a parent there. The beautiful thing about Melissa is she is the one that makes those kids forget that very fact.

58

Chapter 6

My Son

Me in the 1st base box and Jay-Michael getting ready to run free on the bases.

My Life at The Mitch: A Little League Baseball Story

I think all fathers worth their salt always try to pass on what they are passionate about along to their son's. My number one passion has always been baseball. My father passed his love of the game on to me and I felt it only natural to try and pass that love of the game on to Jay-Michael. I feel the high tech age we live in has taken away from the majesty of the game. Every three years players seem to hop from team to team leaving fans to constantly adjust to the new faces. Local commentators and reporters have been taken over by cable networks and bloggers. I can recall my only resource to a Red's game would be sitting on the porch with my dad, a couple of mason jars full of ice water, and listening to Marty Brennaman and Joe Nuxhall on the radio. It was up to those two men to paint the visual of what was happening. Listening to a game on the radio is an experience that fathers and sons don't really enjoy anymore. What father's don't realize is they are missing a grand opportunity to bond with their son's. The beauty of radio is you are forced to talk about other things at some point in the game, with your conversation's only being interrupted by Marty yelling, "...And there's a drive to deep center field!" Dad and I would both pump our fist with joy then resume whatever we were talking about on a warm summer's night. My dad was more responsible for passing that style of the game along to Jay-Michael. Even with the onset of cable television my dad always listened to the game on the radio. He would turn the T.V. on, turn the volume all the way down and crank up Marty and Joe on the radio. One of dad's favorite players to watch play was an unknown outside of the Cincinnati, a shortstop named Pokey Reese. Each time Pokey would make a great play dad would always exclaim, "How 'bout that Pokey." Jay-Michael was about 4 years old at this time and he would sit with me on the couch and watch the game. Papaw's exclamation for Pokey became so commonplace that each time he would make even the most routine of plays Jay-Michael would run into his papaw's room and scream, "How 'bout that Pokey papaw?" The love of the game provides those moments. My father and I had successfully passed it on.

Jay-Michael was a tiny little boy. He had a bad birthday by little league standards and he would be eight years old his entire nine year old year. His mother was fairly insistent on him playing minor league ball out of fear that he would get hurt playing with eleven and twelve year old boys. After weeks of trying to convince her that he would be better off playing little league she agreed to let him join the team. Jay-Michael thought he was in the big leagues. He was playing at "The Mitch" instead of the dusty minor league field that sits behind Mitch Stadium. His nine year old year Jay-Michael would get his two innings and one at bat like most other nine year olds. I would coach all of my boy's every at bat of the game. After each pitch there was always some sort of knowledge I would want to teach them from the first base coaching box. However, each time Jay-Michael came to the plate I would lose all my coaching instincts and just become a nervous parent. God bless him he would try so hard but he was just overpowered by the older players pitching. Since the Braves were always the team to beat that meant that the other team would always throw their top twelve year old against us. When Jay-Michael would step in the box my only thought was "Please don't hit him, please don't hit him." I knew that Jay-Michael was one bean ball away from being shipped back down to the minor's by his mother. More often than not Jay-Michael would go down swinging each time but still amazed the stands by making defensive plays with his eight year old frame. Once while playing second base, Jay-Michael decided to cover the bag when the runner at first attempted to steal. Our catcher, who had a cannon, threw the ball to second base without realizing who was covering. A broken nose and two black eyes were the only scenario that I could think of as the outcome of this play. Jay-Michael stood his ground and by the grace of God stopped the ball in its flight with his glove. After the inning was over Dan explained to Jay-

My Life at The Mitch: A Little League Baseball Story

Michael that he was never to do that again. "But Dan", my son said, "the shortstop wasn't covering the bag." He was right, he wasn't. My boy was learning and a tragedy avoided all on the same play.

Jay-Michael finally got his first hit about five games into the season. It was a little blooper hit down the right field line. Instead of running the hit out or making a turn to second Jay-Michael ran to the bag and with about 2 feet to go jumped on top of the first base bag. I don't think a father has ever been more proud of their son as I was at that moment. As each pitch was thrown after his at bat I kept a close eye on the ball. They were using the same ball that Jay-Michael got his first hit with. How was I going to get this baseball? It was Jay-Michael's first hit. I had to have it. For the next two outs I was praying that no foul ball be hit. My prayers were answered. As is custom in every baseball game ever played when the last out is made the ball is rolled to the pitcher's mound. Strike three was called and the ball was rolled back to the mound. As I walked back to our third base dugout I saw the ball, Jay-Michael's ball, laying there next to the rubber. Like a thief in the night, I looked around and saw that nobody was looking. In a split second the ball found its way from the dirt of the pitcher's mound to the inside of my pocket. As our team took the field our pitcher hollered at the umpire that he needed a ball. The home plate umpire, Scott Milum, looked briefly for the game ball and then reached in his bag to give our pitcher a new one. I had pulled it off, the ball was with its rightful owner. Upon reflection, Scott's attempt to look for the ball seemed to be a put on. He understood how I was feeling, thanks Scott.

The only other highlight Jay-Michael had that year came against the Reds. We were facing the flame throwing, lefthander Crit Stender. Crit was a twelve year old all-star pitcher for the Reds. At the time he was the hardest throwing pitcher in the league. We were down 2-1 in the bottom of the sixth with a runner on second base. It was Jay-Michael's turn at bat and I was already thinking about what I was going to say to Jay-Michael when he made the last out. I just knew I had to put a positive spin on it. You never want a young kid to make the last out in a close game. The first pitch came and I think Jay-Michael swung as the catcher was throwing the ball back to Crit. The next pitch blazed right down the middle as Jay-Michael jumped out of the way as if he was trying to avoid sniper fire. One more pitch to go and I could give my son the loving words that I had came up with. Crit's next pitch was a curveball. A curve ball? To an eight year old? Why on earth would you slow it down for an eight year old? It missed for ball one. Crit later shook off about 3 pitches and that told me it wasn't his idea to throw a curveball. Crit had the mentality that he would finish this gnat off with his fastball. Jay-Michael somehow managed to foul off about 5 fastballs, just barely getting a piece of two of them. My little eight year old had worked the count full against a twelve year old all-star. The last pitch of the at bat was a gasser on the outside corner. Jay-Michael checked his swing, ball four. "GREAT A.B. JAY-MICHAEL", screamed Dan from the dugout. Me being the proud dad, didn't say a word. I was speechless. If only this eight year old really knew what a great effort he just gave. Our lead-off batter came to the plate next and ripped a double to right-center field scoring both runs, game over. After the game, we as coaches like to give our speeches about what the boy's did right and what they did wrong. Dan's speeches usually involve some kind of life lesson. He will usually tie together the way the kids played with how they will perform in other area's later on in life. Mick's speeches tend to ramble on and on and inevitably testing the attention span of our young players. My speeches usually last about thirty seconds. They kind of sound like this."You did well", as I point to one player. "You did bad", as I point to another player and so on. After we are done with our speeches the three of us briefly put our heads together and decide who gets the "game ball." More often than not we just take a baseball out of our bucket of balls to give to the kids. As I finished up my final thoughts Dan took it upon himself to give out the game ball. He said, "Without a doubt we wouldn't have won that game without Jay-Michael's at bat." Dan gave Jay-Michael a "congratulations" and then tossed him the game ball as the rest of the boys cheered. My little eight year old got his first game ball and I didn't have any input on who should get it. Sleep was the only thing that could erase the smile from my face that day. The year came and went and Jay-Michael gathered a couple of more hits. That year was basically a learning experience for him and get used to playing with the big boys. At the end of the year he would be selected to the all-star team which was his first of five.

Jay-Michael's ten year old year came and went without much fanfare. He had improved from a year before and played some junk time at shortstop in preparation for the following year. During his first year he was just happy to be there. You could tell that he was loving whatever time he spent on the field and tried his hardest each and every time he played. About midway through his ten year old year I began noticing signs that he was putting way too much pressure on himself. If he struck out in one at bat it would ruin him for the rest of the game. If he made an error in the first inning he wouldn't forget about it until the third inning of the following game. All in all though Jay-Michael had another good year and was selected as an all-star again. However I found myself battling with him more and more often about being so hard on himself. I would always try to coach him up when something went wrong and buy the end of the year he was having none of it. All-Stars came as a good relief for me since I wasn't coaching. I was able to "enjoy" the games from the stands instead of battling with my son about a play that may have gone wrong. I realized that I needed to put a stop to it because I wanted my son to keep the love of the game. In a flash two years had flown by and his little league career was halfway over. During the offseason though Little League changed its birthday rules and the change added an extra year on to Jay-Michael's little league playing days. So in essence, his eleven year old year would just turn into his second ten year old year.

By the time his second ten year old year had came around Jay-Michael was developing into a pretty good ball player. From now on we will refer to this time as his ten year old year so I don't have to keep saying his second year as a ten year old year. A funny thing began to happen though. Jay-Michael was beginning to hate me. Before the game and after the game we had the normal father/son relationship. It's as if a switch went off in him that triggered once he step foot between the foul lines. I would yell at the other kids on the team as if they had done something horrible yet they all loved me. I would look at Jordan Kinney and yell, "Jordan, are you retarded?" I would look at Bryer Brewer for no reason and say "Bryer, you're the ugliest kid I have ever seen." I would look at Casey Saunders and basically accuse him of being the dumbest kid ever born into this world. They all kept loving me though. Granted, I wasn't serious any time I said these things to the boys. They knew I was joking. Whenever I tried to correct any of their mistakes I would usually start it off with some sort of insult. For whatever reason this is a tool that I have been given that helps me relate to our boys on the team and it works. They know I mean them no harm. They know I love them and their parents know I love them too. Never has Bryer's mom came up to me and asked why I called her son ugly. It's just a weird way we have of ripping on each other out of fun. With that in mind, if Jay-Michael would make an error or strike out I would always start off by saying, "Now I'm not getting on you" or "You had the right idea in mind". Even that didn't seem to be working. Whenever Jay-Michael would pitch for us Mick made it clear that I was to have no interaction with him at all. This bothered me but I understood why he did that. With Jay-Michael you could see the potential of him being a fairly good pitcher if only he could overcome the expectations he put on himself. To this day I don't know what happened to make him act this way. Every

65

so often his being mad at me would make me mad at him. Am I the only father this has happened to? If you combined his newfound hatred for me with the unrealistic pressure he put on himself it made for a volatile situation. When he pitched, if he didn't start off well it usually meant a pretty long day. So basically I spent his entire ten year old year ignoring Jay-Michael and passing my time by continually ripping on the other kids. It really bothered me that I couldn't interact with Jay-Michael in the same way that I did the other boys. Like I said though, after the game was over he was loving me again and we could talk about anything that happened during the game.

 During the regular season Jay-Michael was our shortstop and pitched for us whenever his turn came. So naturally when all-stars came around he expected to pitch when his turn came up. He was in for a shock when he realized he wouldn't be pitching at all during the all-star season. I tried to explain to him that his attitude was what was keeping him from taking the hill. I don't think he accepted that though and you could tell that his disappointment affected his play. His ten year old all-star team was a group of boys that were all good athletes and over achieved themselves to the state finals in Weston, West Virginia. Had they won the championship game against Jefferson County they would've earned a berth in the Tournament of Champions held at Mitch Stadium as the representative for West Virginia. This was a big deal for all the boys because the Tournament of Champions make all the kids feel like they are playing on a big league level. First you have the pleasure of playing on the finest little league field in the entire United States. Then the production that is put on by Paul Billups and 100's of volunteers is phenomenal. The games are all televised with play by play announcers on closed circuit television. The games are also broadcast on-line and can be listened to from anywhere in the world. Every three innings the ground crew comes out and changes the bases and drags the infield. The lists of activities put on by the

66

tournament are endless. From opening day ceremonies that include a parade and guest speaker that will normally be a former big league ball player, to the championship game and the fireworks display that follows. It was a huge deal for our boys to be able to play in front of the hometown fans. It was a game that our boys fell short in. Our boys played their tails off but we lost a heartbreaker.

 The following week was the Tournament of Champions and Jay-Michael's team still got to ride in the parade as a show of appreciation from "The Commish" and the community for what their team had achieved. As I sat in the truck our boys were riding in, waiting for the parade to start, I kept hearing kids hollering "Jay-Michael, Hey Jay-Michael." I got out of the truck to see what was going on and the kids that were hollering for him were the kids from Jefferson County. He had made friends with some of the kids on the team that beat us a week earlier. They were all asking him to ride in the truck with them. One of the coaches for Jefferson County came up to me later that day and asked if I was Jay-Michael's dad. I told him that I was and he said, "Well let me tell you something about your son." "Oh no", I thought, "What has he done." He told me that my son had came up to him and said the if he had to lose the state tournament and the right to play in the Tournament of Champions he was glad he lost to them because he had made some good friends on their team. No home run ball he would later hit in his career could've made me prouder of him than I was at that moment. This coach also took a liking to my grandfather that was there for opening ceremonies. My grandfather, Dick Griffith, dressed in a Cincinnati Reds outfit from head to toe. Where he got this uniform I don't know and why he wore it I don't know. As the day went on, it soon circulated through "The Mitch" that the oldest living Cincinnati Red was at the stadium. I think my grandfather denied it the first few times he was questioned about it but after a while he decided to let the legend grow. Before too much longer I was watching my grandfather signing autographs and taking pictures with people. I just wonder how many people still have those autographs.

Jay-Michael's eleven year old year ended up being one for the record books. Actually, I guess I should say that his eleven year old year ended up being one for the rule books. During regular season Jay-Michael had his usual year full of almost homeruns, excellent fielding and base running, and surprisingly he developed into a pretty good pitcher for us. About halfway through the season he learned how to throw a knuckleball. Mick would let him throw it about once or twice a game. After seeing the effect it had on the batters it slowly became Jay-Michael's number one pitch. Unfortunately, he would have enough mental setbacks during the regular season that would make Mick reluctant to pitch him at the start of all-stars. In his first appearance on the mound during all-stars, Mick felt it best to move Jay-Michael to the mound in the sixth inning of a game we had well in hand. My son toed the rubber and even from my right field seat you could see the dancing of his knuckleball after it left his hand. The combination of his knuckle, fast, and curveball resulted in three up and three down. Mick was thrilled over Jay-Michaels performance and Jay-Michael's confidence was at an all-time high.

Jay-Michael was next on the hill against Mason County. Before the game Mick came and asked me what I thought about Jay-Michael taking the ball for the game. I gave him an honest answer and told him I didn't think he was ready. Dan Brody also voiced the same opinion. So Mick had just received two "No' votes against Jay-Michael pitching that day. To Mick's credit, he went searching for a third opinion. He went to Jay-Michael and asked him if he wanted to pitch. Without hesitation, which is what Mick was looking for and Jay-Michael said yes. Jay-Michael pitched an ok game that day but needed to be relieved by our flamethrower, Caleb Meade. In little league baseball they have a pitch count that you have to abide by.

68

Matthew Cisco

For eleven and twelve year olds you can't go over 85 pitches. Jay-Michael had not, he was pulled in time to allow Mick to use him in the next game if need be. Unfortunately for us though, we had to use all of Caleb's pitches to win the game. The district championship was set. C-K All Stars v. East Huntington All-Stars.

It was the worst day of my life. I had to work that day so I was unable to attend the biggest game in my son's career. I made everyone I knew that had a cell phone promise they would call me with continual updates. I would get calls from his mom at the end of each half inning. "He's doing great, where up 1-0". "He's battling his tail off, we're up 2-0." "You'd be so proud of him Matthew, we're up 4-0". "The boys are playing so good behind him Matthew, we're up 5-0." About 20 minutes went by and I hadn't heard anything from her. I was starting to get nervous so I called and it went to voice mail. I waited about 5 minutes and called again, straight to voice mail.

I work for the Kenova Police Department so I'm around radio conversations from all different jurisdictions in our area. About the time I was going to call Melissa I hear come across the scanner, "All units respond to Kenova Avenue. We have a disturbance involving parents at a baseball game." Somehow in my heart of hearts I knew that Melissa was right in the middle of it. This also meant that for her to be in the middle of it someone had wronged her boy in some way. Keep in mind this is the same woman that I said had an angelic soul unless she felt someone wronged her boy. Earlier that year Melissa was working the concession stand during one of Jay-Michaels games. Jay-Michael had a rough day that day and in his last at bat he ripped a bullet up the middle for a base hit. The helmets the kids wear at Mitch Stadium have facemasks on them. I have a tendency to grab those facemasks when I'm talking to the boys. I grabbed his facemask and began pumping him up. "That's it bubby! Don't

69

ever stop believing in yourself. You are capable of anything if you just keep a good attitude." I was trying to build my son up. I guess from the concession stand perspective though it looked like I was ripping his butt to shreds right there on the field. Melissa had climbed through the window of the concession stand and walked in an irate trot towards our dugout where she waited for me until the inning was over. She was more than ready to unleash her wrath upon me until she finally found out that I was saying good things to our son.

Well, Jay-Michael was pitching a good ball game and the team was playing well behind him. It was in the fifth inning and Jay-Michael was getting near his pitch total that would mean he would have to leave the game. The only problem was, the pitch total that Mick had and the pitch total that the press box had were two different numbers. Jay-Michael walked the last batter he legally faced. Instead of the press box bringing to Mick's attention the fact that Jay-Michael had went over the pitch count, they allowed him to continue on to the next batter. The official score keeper and umpire were both aware he was over the limit yet both failed to inform Mick who had an incorrect total and thought he was still fine to pitch. Jay-Michael threw the next pitch and time was immediately called. East Huntington's coach walked to the umpire and said he wanted to protest the game because Jay-Michael threw an illegal pitch. Common sense would tell most people to just erase the pitch from the count, bring in a new pitcher and let the kids win or lose a game on the field instead of in the rule book. Well, that's what common sense would say anyway. Rumor has it that "the top umpires" in our district even called Williamsport with the dilemma and they ruled that C-K was to lose the ballgame. Our boys were devastated. Melissa's boy had been done wrong, look out to those who got in her way. She called me on the phone to explain all this to me. I was in shock and disbelief when she told me what all was going on. She said, "Matthew, can you come out here please and take care of this?"

70

Matthew Cisco

I was at work some 45 minutes away but it felt like an eternity. I couldn't help her with the rage she was feeling and I couldn't help my son who had pitched his heart out only to have a game taken away from him by adults on a technicality. The rulebook was changed the following year to avoid such an outcome. So my son has his own rule in the little league rulebook. We played in the consolation game and won that game and we represented our district in the state tournament as the "runner-up."

Jay-Michael celebrated his 12th birthday while we were in Princeton, West Virginia for the eleven year old state tournament. His mother came up with the idea to have his birthday party at the Princeton Devil Rays field. They are the minor league affiliate of the Tampa Bay Rays. She had it set up to where each of the kids on our all-star team got to run out onto the field with a Princeton Ray when the line-up was announced. Jay-Michael also got to sit on the field and watch the players warm up and members of the grounds crew took him into the dugout to get autographs from all the players. I would have to say that will be his best birthday party he will ever have. All provided by his mother. During the game we sat underneath the stands behind home plate. There we met a gentleman by the name of Larry Pickering. He had pitched for the Mets in the late 60's yet I have been unable to find out any information on him. I can assume only that he was in spring training for the Mets for a few years but never made the big club. He took an instant liking to Jay-Michael and he talked with him for the entire game. He had my son hanging on every word that he said. He would tell Jay-Michael stories of his days when he faced Hank Aaron and Pete Rose and what tough outs they were. My son was in awe of him. He briefly left to go get Jordan Kinney and Billy Evans to tell them about this superstar of days past that was sitting next to him. Jay-Michael told him that he was going to pitch the next day and Mr. Pickering gave him pointers for the next two hours. "What's your number one pitch", he asked in his Dominican accent. Jay-Michael told him his bread and butter pitch

71

was his knuckleball. Mr. Pickering was thrilled to find out he wasn't "ruining" his arm by throw curve balls at such a young age. "What you need to do when you throw the knuckleball is this", Mr. Pickering said while running his fingernails in the middle of the seams on the baseball. He said that if you loosen up the seams just a little bit that it will add more dance to the knuckleball. After a couple of hours spent with Mr. Pickering, Jay-Michael got him to autograph a baseball and thanked him for all the pointers.

The next day I watched my son warm up in the bullpen before the game going through his usual routines. I sat out in right field as far away from him as possible while still being able to see the game. His mother and I both occupied the same picnic table for the entire game. We sat there together partly to get away from everyone else that was there and partly due to the fact that that was as close as our nervousness would allow us to get to the field while our son was pitching. I was nervous for our son. This was the semifinals of the state tournament and up to this point our boy hadn't given up an earned run. With two outs to go in the first inning I noticed Jay-Michael stepping off the mound and messing with the ball. I knew what he was doing. He was scratching the seams just like Mr. Pickering had told him to. Now I will grant you that it probably didn't actually make a difference in his knuckleball but in the mind of a newly turned 12 year old it made all the difference in the world. From that point on I knew he would be unhittable. He struck out 9 batters, walked two and gave up only one earned run. I should tell you that earned run came at the hands of a blown call at first base but that's neither here nor there. The only reason I bring that up is because at the time I was afraid that would be all it would take to get Jay-Michael out of his grove. The scratching of the seams had a magical power that day though and he struck out the next batter he faced. We went on to lose the championship game the following day but it was still a magical run. Jay-Michael had started the all-star season as a pitching afterthought and ended it being one of the top

72

pitchers on the team.

 After Jay-Michael threw his knuckleball gem against the Elkins All-Star team he was so excited to go back to the Devil Rays field and tell Mr. Pickering all about it. The Rays had a game scheduled that evening but it had been raining off and on all day long. When we got to the field you could see the heartbreak on Jay-Michael's face when he realized the game was canceled and he wouldn't be able to tell his new friend about how well he had done. That was the only time we saw Mr. Pickering but he left a tremendous impact in the mind of a 12 year old boy. Thank you Mr. Pickering for the time you spent with my son that evening and thank you Mom for giving your boy the birthday party that every boy dreams about.

Jay-Michael celebrates his 12th birthday with the Princeton Rays

Chapter 7

The Perfect Season

(L-R Sammy Brody, Jordan Kinney, Bryer Brewer, Jay-Michael Cisco)
This pose was stolen from an old Big Red Machine picture

Matthew Cisco

It was the spring of 2008 and we had started our daily practice schedule for the C-K Braves. Each year I tell Mick at the start of a new year that we are going to win the league and go undefeated. Each year Mick gets upset by my predictions and fears that my confidence in our boy's will somehow jinx their performance on the field. More often than not I have been correct on my championship predictions but never on perfection. Knowing the talent we had coming back I felt that it was possible to not lose a league game all year long. We had Jay-Michael, Bryer Brewer, Jordan Kinney, and Sammy Brody as our key twelve year olds that were returning for their last year. I was hoping that this, their final year, would be one that they would all enjoy.

Jay-Michael and I would talk daily about the upcoming season. I would stress to him on a daily basis about enjoying his final year. I had been battling with him on the field for almost three years to this point. I tried to get the point across to him that he should have fun and enjoy this year no matter the outcome of any game and regardless of whatever may go wrong at points during the season. In reality it was a plea from me to have him loosen up a little. I wanted to enjoy this year with him. I wanted to have the fun with him that I have with other boys on the team. I let him know that I decided that he was to have free reign on the base paths. He had became smart enough on the bases to the point that he could pick and chose whatever he wanted to do and whenever he wanted to do it. It was like setting a wild horse free. After he received this dose of freedom you could tell that he was itching for the season to get started. As a team, we usually start practices about two weeks earlier than other teams. Like I mentioned before, Mick likes to practice the boy's every day. If we don't have a field to practice on we make one. If we don't have our field scheduled for a day we convert the inside of a running track into a baseball field. We've practiced on fields, in dirt lots, and indoors at basketball gyms. We've even held a practice in a parking lot before. I think if Mick had his way he would practice our kid's on gravel if he had to. Our practices may sometimes seem liked chaos but it is a controlled chaos. Coaching is always being done with every kid at all times. Never will you see one of our boys sitting on his glove while the other kids are practicing. I'll have a group hitting on the tee. Mick will have a group working on the mound. Dan will have a group taking infield. Plus you add in the occasional father or grandfather and it all makes for a very constructive practice.

During this year I felt that it was important to make the game fun again for some of the boys. Year in and year out they have been doing the same thing over and over and over again. So now when I hit infield to them I made a game out of it. I would start hitting ground balls to third base and move my way towards first base. I'd have the kids start off by throwing home, then to first and follow that up by having them turn two. At the start of the round the ground balls would be hit easy enough that the kids wouldn't have a problem fielding it. At the start of the round I would tell the boys that if they made a complete round of infield without an error I would buy them all pizza. So you could imagine the excitement they would be feeling when it got down to the last one or two boys. I don't know about you but buying pizza for thirteen kids can be fairly expensive so when it got down to the last few boys I would try and hit it in between them to where they couldn't make a play. Sometimes as the end neared I would move Jordan into second base and hit a screamer to him that any grown man would dive clear of. Every so often despite my plans the boys would pull off a perfect round of infield. Gloves would be tossed in the air, kids would be cheering and high fiving each other. They all would act as if they had just won the Little League World Series. Just so you know I still owe those boys pizza.

After we were done playing that game I would turn infield into some sort of a baseball trivial pursuit game. I would test their knowledge of the game. If

76

any of the boys got an answer right there reward would be that they would be allowed to leave the field and come catch in. Standing beside me while I hit infield was the reward. Can you believe that? These kids took to it though and it kept them more aware during practice. I kept practice moving though. As I was asking these questions I would still be hitting balls to random parts of the field and the kids still had to make the play even if they got the answer right to come stand by me. I would usually start the round off with a question like, "Who was the power hitting catcher for the Homestead Grey's?" The answer of course is Josh Gibson. He was a power hitting catcher in the old Negro leagues. I would ask the question because I knew that Jay-Michael would be the only kid that knew it due to his love of the history of the game. "Bruiser, go to third", I would tell our catcher. I gave Christian Palmer the nickname of "Bruiser" because it was a given that he would get hit by a pitch when he batted at least once a game. The kid doesn't crowd the plate or lean his elbow over the strike zone either. I honestly feel that he wears some sort of magnet that attracts the ball. So Jay-Michael would leave shortstop and come catch in. This was the fun time for me in practice because once I had him there with me we would start messing with the other players. "Who is the all-time homerun leader that cheated to break the record", I would ask. "Barry Bonds", would be screamed from all the way out in centerfield. It was our star centerfielder Jordan Kinney. I would get the same answer about 5 seconds later from our third baseman. I would act like I didn't hear Jordan and say, "Ok Superstar, come on in to catch. Bub you go back to short." Superstar is the nickname I gave to Brandon Harmon. Really I don't know why I started calling him that. This kid is a walking encyclopedia full of baseball stats and player bio's. Later in the year Brandon would develop the most wicked curveball I have ever seen in little league. I am not a fan of curve balls at the little league level but watching Brandon throw his was a thing of beauty. Jordan would always get mad and throw his glove down because I very rarely acknowledged his answers. This would always make

My Life at The Mitch: A Little League Baseball Story

Jay-Michael laugh and you haven't heard anything more priceless than my son when he gets tickled over something. I tried my hardest always to think of a question that would guarantee each kid got to stand by me at least once. "Sammy, what's your dad's name", I would ask. "Dan Brody", screamed Jordan. Without even answering I would say, "That's right Sammy. Come on in to catch." All the kids would be laughing and Jordan would be throwing his hat on the ground and hating me with each passing question. If I were having fun with the kid that was catching in I would ask a question that I knew would stump them but to keep Jordan from quitting the team I would not pretend like I didn't hear him and let him come in to catch. However, the very next question would be something like, "What is the name of the position that throws the ball to the catcher?" Everyone would answer. "Gosh Matt", would be Jordan's reply after his five second stint of catching in. The catcher's mitt would be slammed to the ground and off he would run to centerfield. The whole time Jordan would be swinging his arms wildly as he complained about how unfair I was. It was a beautiful sight. Jordan's reactions to my treatment of him made it all worthwhile and assured the fact that I would pick on him as often as possible.

During these practices I came to a realization. We didn't have any characters on our team. Gone was Big Trev. Gone was Jake Adams. I had become the character on the team. It was up to me to keep all the boys loose. I relished this role. It made me feel like I was playing again. In my playing days I used to do silly things like draw a tic-tac-toe board in the sand at first base. Sometimes it would go ignored. Other times the opposing first baseman would play the game with me. Each inning we would mark our one "O" or "X". In between innings I would do my M.C. Hammer dance as the music was being played over the P.A. Our team only had one dancer on it this year and that was Mason Brubeck. He was our "rookie" and Jay-Michaels younger brother. If music was being played you could rest assured that if the game wasn't going on he would at least be bobbing his head to the beat. I was enjoying my newfound role so much that I almost contemplated moving back to the dugout. Jay-Michael and I were getting along so well in practice I felt the move would be fine.

 The season got underway and I took my rightful place in the coach's box at first base. Jay-Michael was our leadoff man. Within two pitches of the new season I heard coming from the dugout, "Don't drop bats!" I quickly re-thought my idea about leaving the safety of the coach's box and decided it was best that I stayed put. Jay-Michael would get on base his very first at bat of the year and I reminded him of the freedom he had on the base paths. I thought he would wait one or two pitches. The first pitch crossed the plate and off to the races he went, safe. Mick is more of a station to station coach. He likes to play it safe. Dan is the same way screaming, "BACK!" from the dugout regardless if our runner is dancing off the bag or not. I told Jay-Michael to do what he felt was best and live with whatever happened. I explained to him that if he were smart then his steals would be successful at least 90% of the time. I was wrong though. He was picked off only once during the year so he exceeded what I thought he was capable of. When Bryer would get on base I would tell him that he had four pitches to get to third base. He had the freedom to decide what pitches he ran on but knew he had only four pitches to do it in. I felt that this made it entertaining for the parents to watch and made it more fun for the boys. Our fastest boy on the team was Jordan Kinney. When he got on first he would always ask me if he could steal. I would always tell him no and to wait on a passed ball to advance. I know this may not make sense to anyone since he was the fastest on the team. What you need to understand about Jordan is he ran like he had ten pounds of mud caked to his cleats. If he were to unleash himself there is no way he could've been thrown out. Every so often I would let Jordan attempt a steal and more often than not he would get thrown out. This would always be followed by me walking back to the dugout and feeling the burn from the stare that Mick and Dan were giving me. If you put this kid in the outfield there is no ball that he can't track down. If you put him on first base then you better pray for a single and two wild pitches or else he wasn't going to score. Regardless of what happened during a game that year I never was really worried about the outcome because of what I heard coming from the dugout.

You'll recall that my little league coach wouldn't allow us to chatter for the longest time. Well, teams at C-K don't chatter while they're in the field anymore. They chatter while their own team is at bat. It's the complete opposite of the way it was when I played. Actually, they don't really even "chatter". They sing songs. "We want a single, just a little single, S.I.N.G.L.E. single, single, single." This song continues until every possible type of hit is covered. "G double O.D.E.Y.E. good eye good eye" or "G double O.D.C.U.T. good cut good cut good cut HEY" were just a few of the musical melodies you would hear coming from the Braves dugout. Mr. Rutherford would surely be rolling in his grave at such an abomination occurring during a baseball game. The kids on the team eventually tired of singing these songs over and over again so they became a little more creative yet lazy at the same time. They wanted to come up with new chants to sing but didn't put the time into thinking of something on their own or that even related to baseball. As the games wore on little variations of the chants they had sang before started to be heard. After that point it just became ridiculous. Midway through the season you could hear Jordan and Jay-Michael in their high pitched voice and Bryer providing the bass when they sang the "Free Credit Report Dot Com" jingle that everyone has seen on T.V.

What everyone needs to know about Bryer Brewer is that he is a twelve year old boy with a voice of a 65 year old smoker. I have never heard a

80

kid with such a low voice as his. "High Matt", in his deep baritone voice he would say. "High Bryer", I would say back to him failing to match his bass levels. One of my favorite qualities about Bryer was that you always knew when an error was coming from him or when he wasn't going to throw a strike because as soon as the ball left his hand you would hear him yell, "Ahhhh!" He and Jordan were my two favorite to rip on during a game. "Shut up Matt" or "You're such a dork" was about the only things Bryer said to me that entire year. The kid was always honest with me about what he was thinking. I never worried about not getting an honest answer from Bryer. There would be times I would visit him on the mound when he was having a tough time and I would try to build his confidence or ease whatever pressure he was putting on himself. "Who's the best pitcher in the league Bryer? Who would I want on the mound for me right now?" He knew I was building him up but he replied with what he thought was an honest answer, "Caleb Meade, Matt.", the hard throwing right hander for the Pirates. I would laugh and walk back to the dugout and Bryer would usually strike out the next batter to get out of the jam.

 I was coaching one of our boys, Thomas Napier, at first after he had gotten a hit. As I congratulated Thomas I heard this blood curdling cry come from our dugout. It was Jordan. I thought he had hurt himself or had finally driven Dan over the edge. I saw that other kids were laughing so I assumed that he was fine and no harm had been done to him. I later asked Jay-Michael what he was doing and he told me that he was doing a scene out of a movie. The following inning, I made Jordan play out this scene again for me. It was a dead on impression of Will Ferrell in "Anchorman" after his dog Baxter was killed. I had never seen anything funnier in a little league dugout. I made him do this impression about ten more times that year. The boys were playing lose and midway through the year we were still undefeated.

 Our record was still perfect but Jay-Michael was starting to feel a weight on his back. He had gone his entire little league career without hitting a home run. He would ask me what the feeling was like to hit one and I would describe it as best I could. I knew that he had it in him to hit one but I always wondered if the day would ever come. I described it to him as the best feeling in all of sports. I told him that after his first home run it would feel like he was floating around the bases. It made me somewhat nervous telling him about all these feelings because I didn't want it to be a letdown to him if he never hit one. I realized that the odds may be stacked against him because we always faced the other team's best pitcher.

District Tournament Champion Ceredo-Kenova Braves

Matthew Cisco

Front row L-R Ryan Edwards, Mason Brubeck, Dana Maynard, Jay-Michael Cisco, Brandon Harmon, Christian Palmer
Second Row L-R Casey Saunders, Jordan Kinney, Thomas Napier, Alex Roy, Sammy Brody, Bryer Brewer
Coaches L-R Dan Brody, Matthew Cisco, Mick Osburn

For whatever reason, our district decided to hold the district tournament in the middle of our regular season. For all the years that I have coached there the tournament had been held after the regular season was over and before all-star play began. Mick, Dan, and I decided we would play out the string without messing up our pitching rotation for our regular season games. I felt that we would win the first game since we were playing a lower seeded team and pack our bags following the second round. Our first game we decided to pitch Jay-Michael. He was having a pretty good game but for the first two innings our kids couldn't hit a basketball had it been thrown toward the plate. Jay-Michael, Bryer, and Sammy Brody all had their home run swings that day which resulted in no hits and 6 pop up's. Being the goofball that Bryer is, at the start of the 3 inning he decided to pick up the game ball as he ran to shortstop, step on the mound and throw a pitch to our catcher Alex Roy. The umpire's saw this and declared Bryer as our new pitcher. It was an incorrect ruling but by this time Mick had went nuts on ALL the boys for Bryer's mistake and I didn't have it in me to argue the ruling. Jay-Michael was out and Bryer was in. Our pitching rotation was shot for the rest of the tournament. We squeaked by a team that we should've beaten by ten runs. Our next game would be against a team from Wayne, WV. There coach was a former teammate of mine from my summer league American Legion days.

We were limited on our options of who we wanted to pitch and for how long we could pitch them. That dilemma put us in a whole and we were trailing this team 5-2 going into the fifth inning with the middle of our order coming to the plate. Somehow we managed to get runners on first and second with two outs with the number nine batter in the lineup coming to the plate. It was our rookie, utility player Mason Brubeck. I thought all the tough at bats we had that inning would be wasted since Mason was overpowered by the pitcher that Wayne had on the mound. Like his older brother four years earlier Mason stood tall and was up to the challenge. He worked the count to full by fouling off a number of tough pitches. The final pitch of his at bat tailed a little bit inside and Mason turned his shoulder into it and took one for the team. Dan Brody was going crazy like he had done four years earlier to Jay-Michael. "GREAT AT BAT MASON", Dan yelled. This brought Jay-Michael, our leadoff hitter to the plate.

The stage had been set for him by his little brother. I hollered at him to be patient and pick one out that he liked. I was hoping that he would hit a gap shot and clear the bases. Once we got Jay-Michael on base it was almost a given that he would score. If Jay-Michael could clear the bases where he could run freely and make something happen we would be up by one run. "Make your shoe laces pop Bubby", I hollered at him. This was the first time I had ever said that to him. Why I said it I don't know. I was repeating what my dad always used to say to me and it just came out without me even thinking about it. Jay-Michael showed absolutely no patience at the plate and ripped away on the first pitch. The pitch was a waist high fastball that was middle in on the plate. PING! "OH MY GOSH", I exclaimed with fatherly glee. I saw the ball rocket off his bat like I had never seen before and he had gotten under it just by a hair. This was no base clearing line drive in the alley. This was a grand slam home run that soared over the left centerfield wall. I can't explain how thrilled I was. My son had just put his team up for good with one swing of the bat and the stands were going crazy. More importantly for me though a monkey was off my sons back. He got to experience the feeling that I had been talking about all year long. It had finally come. The coach for the C-K Dodgers, Scott Milum, would

84

always tell me that Jay-Michael would hit one. I found a comfort in his reassurance but was always nervous that the day would never come. Well that day had finally arrived.

When you hit your first home run you always seem to fly around the bases because you are so excited. You usually don't think to slow down just a little bit and take it all in. Not my boy. He had his home run trot working perfectly that day and almost ran it a little too slow. Afterwards I explained to him that when he gets older if he is fortunate enough to hit a home run he should pick up his trot just a little bit. "Bub," I would tell him, "If you make a home run trot too slow the next time you are up the pitcher may put one in your ear." Nothing was taking me off of this high that I was feeling as a dad. I don't think I ever jumped as high as I did when I saw him hit his first home run. As Jay-Michael was rounding the bases I could hear my cell phone going off in my pocket. I looked and saw that it was my Aunt Jane calling from the right field bleachers. I thought to myself there was no way I could speak with her at that moment. I was too excited to be on the cell phone. I realized that she wanted to share her excitement with me but there was no way I was answering the phone. As he crossed home and was mobbed by his teammates my phone was still blowing up in my pocket. I just let it keep ringing over and over for what seemed like an eternity. I took it out of my pocket after Jay-Michael had made his way to the dugout and looked to see that I had five missed calls all coming from his mother. She was out in the right field seats as well and was wanting to talk with me about what she saw her son just accomplish. I felt it in my best interest to call her back because she could see that I looked at my phone and she would realize I knew it was her. I didn't want to feel the wrath from this angelic woman by snubbing her during her happiest baseball experience to date. As I stood in the coach's box I dialed her phone and without even saying hello I heard, "Oh my gosh! That was awesome! That was awesome! Tell him I love him. Tell him I'm proud of him. Was that not awesome Matthew?" I couldn't even get a word out to her before I heard the first base umpire say, "Cisco, put that phone away. You can't have a cell phone on the field." Like I said, nothing was going to take me off this high. "Got to go Mama", I said as I hung up on her. "My bad", I told the umpire, "That was my son's first home run and his mom just wanted to talk to me about it, she was excited."

Well hanging up on Melissa didn't set well with her during this time. I was the outlet she used to try and get closer to her baby during this happy time. She called me back. I let it ring. She called again. Again, I let it ring. After the third time she called me back I could feel a whole being burned in the back of my head. "Mama", I said, "The umpire won't let me talk on my cell phone while I'm standing out here." I had just barely gotten those words out when I was warned again by the umpire to hang up the phone. If it is an actual rule or not, after being told that this was your sons first home run would you, as an umpire, enforce such a beautiful and harmless violation? This goes back to my dad's theory about the game needing characters. I couldn't see my dad threaten a coach with an ejection after learning that coach's son had just hit his first homerun. Again though, nothing was going to ruin my high. I hung the phone up on my son's mother for a second time in a matter of one minute.

By this time the inning was over and I had made it to the safety of the dugout. When I walked in the dugout I found my son and shook him so hard that he will probably have back troubles when he gets older as a result of my excitement. "I love you Bubby. I bet you didn't feel a thing when you hit it", I said with glee. "I didn't dad. I didn't feel a thing. It was awesome. I don't even remember running the bases", my son said to me. It was the most awesome experience I had ever shared with my son. I found a safe corner of the dugout to hide in where I felt safe to get my cell phone and call his mother. I was talking with his mother about what our son had just accomplished from the safety of my little whole in the dugout. Our team was warming up on the field getting ready for their half of the inning when the unthinkable happened. I looked up and peering around the corner of the dugout was the first base umpire. "I told you Cisco to hang up that phone or else I'm going to toss you out of here", he said with his major league umpire voice. As I was in the middle of the "nothing is going to ruin my high" thought I realized. This guy was on the verge of ruining a magical moment between a son, his mother, his great aunt, his "ganky" and his father. "Why don't you just shut your mouth and call the game Mr. "X"", I said. I felt that a definite tossing was coming at that point but it had to be said. The worst mistake an umpire can make is trying to become part of the game. I gave the benefit of the doubt to him when I had the phone out while I was on the field. Is it really slowing the game or providing a distraction to the players by me standing in the corner of a dugout on the cell phone? I felt something had to be said at that point though. To his credit he didn't toss me. Mick and Dan both told me to shut up and not get tossed after what my son had just achieved. I zipped my lip and kept my mouth shut until after the game. I worked at the same place as the home plate umpire and unfortunately for him he caught all my venting after the game. The game was capped off by Jordan Kinney making a leaping catch to rob a home run to seal the victory. My high had been restored.

Word was getting around that Jay-Michael had developed into a pretty good fast ball hitter. In the semi-final game of the district tournament we played the C-K Dodgers and felt we could sneak by them without using one of our top pitchers, Sammy Brody. We decided to bring in Sammy though for the minimum pitch count that would allow him to pitch in the title game. We were able to get by them fairly easily and the game was highlighted by Sammy's first round tripper of the year. The showdown was set between the C-K Braves and a team from our rival league of

My Life at The Mitch: A Little League Baseball Story

Barboursville, West Virginia.

Another thing had happened that made this dad have pride seeping out of his pores. Jay-Michael was getting a lot of playing time at first base and was doing an outstanding job. He was making all the plays look routine. The high throws that he had to jump and catch while keeping his foot on the bag. The low throws that he was forced to scoop out of the dirt were a thing of beauty. He was carrying on the Cisco legacy at first base. I couldn't have been prouder of my baby boy. Championship day had arrived. As our kids were loosening up I was watching the kid that Barboursville had warming up in the bullpen. He was a junk ball pitcher. I was filled with dread because up to that point Jay-Michael couldn't hit off speed pitches. He was a fastball, gap hitter that was sometimes made to look foolish on a good curveball. I stressed the importance to him of sitting on the fastball but adjusting to the curve just like my dad had taught me. It was a pitcher's duel for the longest time. This junk ball pitcher from Barboursville was taming the bats of the mighty Braves. After three innings we were trailing 3-1. Sammy was pitching his heart out. Two of the three runs that they had scored to that point were unearned. The bottom half of our order would have to step up again for us to come back and win.

The beautiful thing about the C-K Braves is that we truly were a team. Sure we were stacked with our "Fabulous Four" twelve year olds but it was the younger kids that always seemed to step up when they were needed. Our up and coming ten year old, Alex Roy, would always get a hit when we needed it or work extra hard behind the plate preventing runners from advancing at the most crucial time. Alex is still young but you can tell that as he gets older and bigger he will be a force to be reckoned with. Dana Maynard, one of our outfielders, always seemed to make a play or get on base at a most needed time. I gave Dana the nickname "Kellogg" because that was the name of the school that he went to. When Dana first came to

88

our team he was a shy kid that didn't talk to anyone. After I gave him that nickname it seemed to loosen him up and make him feel like a part of the team. It's amazing what a simple nickname can do. Dana can grow up to be President of the United States one day, but to me, he we always be "Kellogg".

Ryan Edwards was another of our younger players that played his heart out and seemed to come up big from time to time. I enjoy coaching Ryan because you will never meet a sweeter kid than him. I deem some kids as "criers" in the league. If they strike out or make an error some kids that age tend to take it too hard on their self and start to cry. I try to stress to our boys that there is no room for crying in baseball unless they are physically hurt. I do this in an attempt to relieve undo pressure that kids this age put on their self. I wouldn't classify Ryan as a "crier." I would call him a "lip quiverer." I think that he fights back his disappointment because he knows that I don't like it when one of our boys cries without being hurt. Watching him try his hardest to hold back the tears will make any hardened heart grow softer. He's one of my favorites because while there have been other kids as coachable as he, there has never been a kid more coachable than Ryan Edwards. As I said before I tend to grab the facemasks of the players helmet when I talk with them. When I do this to Ryan I get carried away and shake his head back and forth while I am speaking with him. For some reason, this kind of concussion inducing behavior makes Ryan smile and relax. It takes different ways to get through to individual kids. That's why I never fault a coach when he coaches one kid different from the other. You often will hear parents complain about why a coach gets on one kid but not the other. I've learned that each of these kids are individuals and you have to treat them as such.

The stage had been set yet again by the bottom of the order. Again, Mason had set the stage for his big brother. As Jay-Michael walked to the

My Life at The Mitch: A Little League Baseball Story

plate I told him something that went against everything I had ever tried to teach him. "Set on the curveball son", I told him. It's hard to all at once change habits that have been built in over a five year period. Jay-Michael disproved this. The first pitch was a curveball. Jay-Michael had gotten out on his front foot but it was a hanging curveball that was heading his way and he had kept his hands back. I swear to you that I saw his eyes widen to a point that I have never seen before. BANG! There it went. I lost track of the ball that was heading to deep leftfield. After I couldn't see it anymore I looked down to see an elderly man running about 100 feet past the left field wall. I can honestly say that I think that ball easily traveled over 300 feet before coming down. I was in awe of the power that was just displayed by my little boy. It was the second career homer of his life and he acted as if it were a normal occurrence for him. His level of confidence was sky high and its height was equaled by his cockiness level. As he rounded shortstop he looked towards the Barboursville bench and threw his arms out as if to say, "What? Are you really trying to throw a curveball by ME? I'm Jay-Michael Cisco, didn't you know that?" Again I had to remind Jay-Michael that once he got older if he showed a pitcher up like that he was liable to find the next pitch he faced in his ear hole. I didn't press the issue though because my son was having the time of his life and we were getting along like best friends on the field. The victory was sealed the following inning with a 1-6-3 double play. A one hopper was hit to Sammy Brody, he turned and fired it to Bryer Brewer who then made a quick, snap throw to Jay-Michael at first base. The rare ground ball double play in little league had been successfully turned. We were district champs. The last time a C-K team had won the district tournament was some 25 years ago when I was twelve years old. We were beaten in the finals by Mick's team, the Reds.

The C-K Braves were looking at the real possibility that they would have a true undefeated season. I never thought we would win the district and my prediction was meant to imply that we wouldn't lose any of our regular season league games. The pressure was on but these kids didn't feel it until the last game of the year. We kept rolling on through the league for the second half of the season and Jay-Michael added a few more home runs to his total of long balls. We were down one player do to a horrific bicycle accident. Thomas Napier was in a single vehicle bicycle wreck on his way home following a practice. He actually had to spend some time in the hospital because he had done internal damage to himself. Once a Brave always a Brave though. Thomas made his triumphant return to the dugout and sat in there with us for the rest of the year. All the kids autographed a ball for him and made a considered effort not to celebrate too much around him out of fear of hurting him. His playing days were over for the year but Thomas still came to each game and we both would sit in the dugout as the Braves were in the field and spit seeds into cups. I was proud of Thomas for still wanting to be around his teammates even though he was on the DL for the rest of the year.

Halfway through the second half of the year is when you start seeing growth in your younger players. All the boys seemed to be playing much better and even little Mason was getting the taste for the long ball. At nine years old he would one hop the wall on a number of occasions. He would look at me and ask, "Babu, do you think I can hit a home run this year?" Babu is the name that he and his sister have called me ever since they were little. They tried to call me "Matthew" but "Babu" is what came out. I have refused to allow them to call me by my actual name since. "I don't know Mason. I never thought I would say this but maybe. If not this year you will for sure get one next year" I replied back to him. An eleven year old for the Dodgers, Chandler Milum, is the only other kid I have seen in our league that had such power at such a young age. The second half of the season flew by. It did so because I was enjoying this time in my sons life and everything was going by so fast. Before I knew it my sons little league career was almost over.

My Life at The Mitch: A Little League Baseball Story

The only team in our league that I worried about playing was the Pirates. If you matched the kids up player by player there was no doubt that we were the better team. However, if the Pirates throw Caleb Meade then that puts the entire matchup in doubt. Caleb had an absolute rifle for an arm and seemed to overmatch our lineup from top to bottom. The only positive we had was that Jay-Michael had early success against Caleb so his confidence was high every time he faced him. The only other bonus I could think of was that Caleb had the same problem so many kids his age have. He put way too much pressure on himself and if one thing went wrong it really tested his confidence. If Caleb was on his game he was unbeatable. The final chapter of the C-K Braves was set in place with the last game of the year being C-K Braves v. C-K Pirates and yes, Caleb Meade would take the ball that day.

Caleb was on that day. His fastball was humming in there at what seemed to be 100 miles per hour. He was hitting his spots. Inside and outside corner on the paint. His curveball was buckling the knees of all our hitters. If he walked someone or an error was made behind him it didn't phase him in the least. That day it seemed Caleb had matured into a big time pitcher. Jay-Michael had early success against Caleb getting a single in his first at bat of the game. Jay-Michael loves to wreak havoc when he is on base and this day was no exception. Jay-Michael got the only hit that inning but somehow managed to score to give us an early lead. Jay-Michael went 3-3 off of Caleb that day with a single, double, and triple. Fortunately for us Caleb ran out of his allotted pitches and was removed from the game. From that point on we cruised to a fairly easy victory but it wasn't in hand until Caleb was forced from the game. He had pitched one heck of a ballgame and a pitching stud was born for our all-star team. The C-K Braves had achieved the unachievable. The first truly perfect season ever recorded at Mitch Stadium.

After the game I was worried about who would get the game ball. It was a true team effort all year long and we had other deserving twelve year olds on our team that had played their last game as a C-K little leaguer. Like Dan five years earlier though I decided to grab the game ball and give it to the player that I felt had the biggest impact on us winning the game without getting input from the other two coaches. I was a little nervous about the decision I came to. I didn't want parents, especially Dan since he coached with us, to think that I had slighted their kid by not giving the game ball to them. We gathered all the kids behind the dugout and prepared them for our postgame speeches. Again, Mick's speech rambled on and was starting to lose the attention of the players. Dan equated what the team had accomplished to a life lesson that should be learned and appreciated and I simply looked at my son and said, "If it wasn't for you we wouldn't have won today. I then looked at the other boys and said, "Sammy you carried us on your back some days. Jordan and Bryer you too have carried us on your back some days but today though I am giving the final game ball of the year to the kid whose back we rode today. I'm giving the game ball to Jay-Michael." Dan looked at me and said, "I couldn't agree with you more." A true baseball purist, without bias, to the very end.

All-Stars is always a fun time of the year for Jay-Michael and I. Sammy, Bryer, and Jordan had all made the all-star team each year with Jay-Michael. It was fun for us though because he got to play with all the other players of the league that got selected to play. It was also fun for everyone else because they didn't have to face Caleb Meade anymore. Now he was on our team. I felt fairly good about our chances. Granted you never really know what kind of teams you are going to face but I felt our boys would make a pretty good run in all-stars. The parents of Chandler Milum and Zack Harvey decided to let their boy's play on the twelve year old team. Both Chandler and Zack are eleven years old. Both are excellent pitchers and both carry a big stick to the plate.

My Life at The Mitch: A Little League Baseball Story

We managed to go undefeated through pool play by riding the arm of Caleb Meade and the timely hitting of Caleb, Billy Evans, Chandler Milum, Jake Wellman, Zack Harvey and all the Braves on the team. During pool play we beat East Huntington. You may recall that it was East Huntington that beat us by a controversial ruling the year earlier so that victory was extra special for Jay-Michael. Once we advanced out of pool play into the elimination rounds we found ourselves facing East Huntington again in the semi-final game. Our boys played well that day and again we came up on the winning side of the scoreboard. A titanic showdown was set up between the C-K All-Stars v. the Barboursville All-Stars in the district finals.   It's a rivalry that has grown over the years. Our boy's played their hearts out in that game but lost in a heartbreaker. As usual it was just one little error or a lapse in judgement that our boys would have and the kids from Barboursville, to their credit, would always seem to take advantage of it. The loss set us up with, you guessed it, East Huntington in the consolation game. The game wasn't really close from the very start. Everyone had depleted all their pitching at this point in the tournament and our pitching and defense really set the stage during the game by making all the routine plays without error. The game was also highlighted by homerun blasts from Caleb Meade and our catcher Jake Wellman. We won the runner up game and were going back to the state tournament for the third year in a row. Jake Wellman would later break his wrist before the state tournament and his loss was felt during our tournament run.

We traveled to Clarksburg, West Virginia for the tournament and our first game was against Pocahontas County. This was a special game for Jay-Michael because Pocahontas County was the county in which his Papaw's cabin is located. Our family has spent a lot of time there and you can really feel dad's presence while in the mountains. Jay-Michael got the home run barrage going by hitting an absolute bomb high into the trees of left center

94

field. Three other kids would hit home runs that game. Jay-Michael also made the best play I have ever seen by a little league shortstop. A blistering ground ball was hit in between short and third. He dove to his right and completely laid out for the ball. Somehow he snagged it, got to his feet and threw a dart to Billy Evans at first base in time for the out. We went on to mercy Pocahontas County. After the game, more people from Pocahontas County came up to congratulate Jay-Michael than people from C-K. They were truly a classy group of kids and parents.

During our second game the kids played the exact opposite of the way they did in the first. Every imaginable way you can think of to make an error we did and our bats fell silent. Our boys and coaches may have overlooked Logan because they were the lowest seed in the bracket and they simply came to play and we didn't. The coaches and parents were sick to their stomachs about the loss but true to the form of a young child, by the time we made it back to our hotel they had put the loss behind them and were already making plans for what they were going to do that evening.

In the first game of the elimination round Mick decided to put Jay-Michael and his knuckleball on the hill. We had advanced out of pool play only playing two games and the first game of the next round we would play the same Logan team that had just beaten us. The first inning started off smoothly and my boy mowed them down in order. That was the highlight of his day though. In the following inning he had the leadoff batter down 0-2 and was on the verge of getting his second strike out of the game. Unfortunately his knuckleball got away from him and he hit the batter. This rattled Jay-Michael and they ended up scoring 2 runs that inning before he worked himself out of the jam. The following inning the flood gates opened. Before I knew it they had hit 2 home runs off my boy. It would've been three after we brought Caleb Meade into the game had Tyler

My Life at The Mitch: A Little League Baseball Story

Robertson not made a spectacular catch robbing a boy of a home run to dead center field. Tyler had mistimed his jump by a split second and draped his waste over the outfield wall. The ball had barely cleared the fence and as it came down Tyler reached out and caught the ball inches away from it hitting the ground on the other side. It was the most amazing robbery of a home run that I have ever seen on any level of baseball. Had camera's been there to record this catch I can promise you they would've ran it on ESPN that evening. I will go so far as to say they would've ended up showing his catch on TV more times than you have seen the old black and white clip of Willie Mays catch. Some say that Willie Mays is the best to ever play. I have news for you though. His catch was the basic "can of corn" catch compared to the snag of Tyler Robertson. It was the story we were going to talk about after we suffered our final defeat and got eliminated after the first game of the second round. We brought Caleb Meade into the game and he held them scoreless for the rest of the game. We somehow managed to scrape two runs across the plate and went into the top of the sixth inning trailing 5-2. Our boys were able to load the bases but at the expense of getting two outs along the way. We were down to our final at bat and our number nine batter was at the dish. That number nine batter was Jordan Kinney. I think Jordan may have gotten one hit during all of all-stars. The last ball he hit on the nose occurred sometime during the first half of the regular season and his confidence at the plate had long since disappeared. The first pitch came to Jordan and he swung about two seconds late. Pitch number two was dealt and Jordan checked his swing for a called ball one. Jordan was even late on his check swing. The third pitch came and it was a bullet on the outside corner. Jordan rocked in his stance and swung with everything he had. "PING"! It might be, it could be, it's gone. The ball cleared the right field wall by about five feet. At no point did the ball get higher than fifteen feet off the ground. It was an absolute rocket shot that he had hit. In the words of Jack Buck, longtime St. Louis Cardinals announcer, I thought to myself, "I don't believe what I just saw." I didn't know what to do so I took off running toward the dugout from my seat beyond the right field wall. I wasn't really sure what I was going to do when I got there except for letting Jordan know how proud his old ball coach was of him. I wasn't able to make it that far. As I was running toward the dugout I ran by the right field bleachers. Doing her best Jimmy "Superfly" Snuka impression Jordan's mother, Vicki Blankenship, came off what seemed like the top bleacher and dove straight for me. Luckily I caught her out of the air and I just stood there, holding her in my arms, both screaming words that neither one of us could understand. It didn't matter though because we were both at least making noises. After carrying her around for what seemed like an eternity I put her down and we just looked at each other without a clue of what to do next. We went on to retire the side in the bottom half of the inning and had completed a remarkable comeback. Again it was proven to Jay-Michael that baseball is a team game. With the seemingly meaningless catch from Tyler Robertson and the out of nowhere power from his longtime Braves teammate Jordan Kinney, Jay-Michael had been bailed out. We lived to fight another day. We made it past the first game in the elimination round. Our next game in the tournament was against Barboursville. Sigh.

Caleb had run out of pitches during the game against Logan and was unable to pitch so we went with eleven year old Zack Harvey. Caleb got the game going by hitting a moon shot deep into the trees behind the left field wall. We jumped out to an early 2-0 lead and Zach was pitching his heart out. Zack eventually ran out of pitches and was forced out of the game. Just like always a harmless error here and there against Barboursville was taken advantage of by their boys. We clung to a one run lead heading into the top of the sixth inning. After another error was made we had one out to go with one man on base. Barboursville's star player was at the plate and you just had that feeling that something bad was going to happen. It did. He went yard over the right field wall and put his team up by one run. It was such a deflating moment for the boys. However we still had a chance though. We got the final out without any more damage and went into the bottom of the sixth trailing by one. Jay-Michael was due up third that inning. Jay-Michael had success against their fire baller earlier in the district round by recording one of the few hits we got against him so I felt his confidence would be high. Our first two batters got out and up to the plate stepped my precious boy. With as fast as their pitcher threw and as hard as Jay-Michael swung the bat I knew that if he hit it right it would go a long way. I had visions of Jay-Michael running around the bases in triumph after tying up the game with a dramatic homerun. Those visions were not meant to be. Jay-Michael took three called strikes and just like that his little league career was over.

My heart broke for all the boys but I was aching for Jay-Michael. I just wanted to give him a hug and tell him how proud I was of him. Our boys were devastated. All of them had tears in their eyes and some even getting sick and throwing up just outside the dugout. They were so close and this game meant the world to them. That's when I heard coming from left field, "Nah nah nah nah, nah nah nah nah, hey hey hey, goodbye." I know what you are thinking. The Barboursville kids were just being kids. They are our rivals and in their immaturity that was the only way they knew how to celebrate. Well, it wasn't the kids that were doing it. It was some of the "adults" that came to root Barboursville on. Chanting that at these distraught twelve year old children? Really? To the credit of some of the kids on the Barboursville team and their manager who's "Heeeeeeeeey! SHUT UP!" quickly snuffed out the chants of some of our rivals.

I wanted more than anything to have my son ride back to the hotel with me. I wanted to recap with him what a magical year he had provided for his father. I didn't even bother asking him to go with me because I knew that he would want to drive back with his mama. Instead I rode back to the hotel with his "Ganky." His Ganky is my mother. The name "Ganky" came from Jay-Michael trying to say "Granny" when he was younger. We both sulked in the pain that Jay-Michael must've been feeling during the car ride back. When I got back to the hotel I went to Jay-Michael's room to talk with him. By this time it was closing in on ten o'clock at night. He wasn't there. His mom said that he and Mason had gone down to the indoor pool that was at the hotel. I opened the door to the pool room and there sat Jay-Michael and Mason, having the entire place to their self, in the hot tub. I sat there and just watched my boy for about five minutes without saying a word wondering what pain he must be feeling. He was smiling and seemed to be relaxing but it wasn't that full smile of his that I had grown accustom to. I took off my shoes, socks and shirt and started to slide my way into the hot tub with him. I soon discovered that children play the game of baseball because it's just that, a child's game. You could tell that Jay-Michael was hurting but not near as bad as the grown up's that went to watch them play. We briefly talked about the game. For the most part though, we talked about things that had nothing to do with baseball.

After sitting in the hot tub for about ten minutes we both felt the need to get out before we melted. Jay-Michael and Mason both went and dove in the pool. I stood near the edge with my toes gripping the side of the pool. "Are you going to do it dad", asked Jay-Michael. He knew that I had a fear of water and never got in a pool. I put my phobia behind me because I felt that by me getting in the pool it would amaze my son and take his mind off the game. I dove in headfirst and came back up to the surface of the water. My heart was beating a million times a minute and I knew that I was either going to drown or have a heart attack in the pool. Jay-Michael was amazed that I had done it. We just swam around in the pool for a few minutes and eventually I began to relax. Before I knew it Billy Evans was in the pool. Then Jordan followed by Bryer. After about ten minutes it seemed the entire team was in the water. Billy started doing cannonballs off the deep end. When I say deep end it is being somewhat misleading.

My Life at The Mitch: A Little League Baseball Story

The "deep end" was actually about five feet of water. Everyone was in awe of how high Billy's splash was when he entered the water. Billy would brag about his splash and the wake that it created as if there were Olympic judges there all holding score cards of 10 in the air. I knew I had about 150 pounds on Billy so I felt that I could really blow their young minds away with a cannonball of my own. I steadied myself on the edge and went for it. Granted I never got to see the size of my splash but I knew what pain I endured to create it. As I entered the water to do my cannonball I sank to the bottom like a 200 pound stone and my butt slammed into the bottom of the pool. "That was awesome Dad. Do it again", yelled Jay-Michael. Billy too was amazed by the splash and laughed with that infectious laugh of his. I couldn't let my son or his buddies down at this point so I had to do it one more time. Off I jumped and crashing into the floor of the pool I went again. All in all I did about ten cannonballs for Jay-Michael and the boys and it was worth every ounce of pain I felt for me to know that my son was proud of his fat dad for creating such a huge, record breaking splash.

By this time it was about eleven o'clock and the pool had been officially closed for about an hour. Some of the kids were starting to worry that someone from the hotel would come and get us in trouble. They were already sick of us being there seeing how all of our boys were running down the halls every night and one of them even broke an elevator. "What are they going to do? Kick us out", I asked some of the boys. "We're leaving tomorrow morning anyway so let's go out in style." After about fifteen more minutes of playing in the pool Melissa came down and had this look of amazement on her face. She couldn't believe what she was seeing either. After about two seconds of her processing I being in the water, her shoes came off and in the water she went. There we were, ex-husband and ex-wife, swimming together in the pool with our son and the rest of the boys, trying to make their last night fun for them. It was truly a night I will cherish forever.

Matthew Cisco

After another thirty minutes of throwing young kids in the air and dunking Jordan to the point of almost killing him we decided that we had had enough. Being the free spirit that Melissa is she decided that it was too early for us all to call it a night. "Why don't we take all the boys out to eat at Denny's", she asked. After we all dried off and got ready to leave it was almost one in the morning. Only a person as crazy as Melissa would think that it was a good idea to take a group of twelve year old boys, who are physically and emotionally exhausted, out to eat at one in the morning. So Melissa, Deena Milum and I all loaded up the kids in our two cars to go have a feast at Denny's.

Anyone that has ever been in a Denny's at that late of an hour will tell you that the top levels of society won't be found in there at that time. This stereotype held true. Off to our right sat four tables of drunken college kids. Off to our left was a man and his date that he had clearly paid for. The capper was what we saw as soon as we walked in. There, at a table, sat about eight nerds that had just come back from watching the newly released Batman movie. It may seem harsh to call people nerds that went and saw that movie. How else would I know where they came from if they weren't all decked out in their batman gear? One guy was dressed head to toe as the Joker. His face was even painted to look like him. This man had to be at least in his early 30's.

Our dorky kids acted as if this guy was in fact the real Joker. They all took pictures with him and got autographs off of him. Our boys though had long forgotten about the game they had just lost and I suppose that was Melissa's intent all along. After trying to keep a group of boys quite while we waited forty-five minutes for our food, we ate and then loaded back into the cars and headed for the hotel. I had the misfortune of riding with Deena, her son Chandler, and a small group of other boys. After the combined ten minute drive to get to and from Denny's Chandler and I were on the verge of coming to blows. I had all intentions of making Deena stop the car so Chandler and I could throw down. She just laughed the whole way back and I thought to myself what a lucky man her husband Scott was for having stayed back at the hotel. We all went back to our rooms and settled in for a well earned sleep. It was as I was laying in bed that it all dawned on me. My little boy's little league career was over. A chapter in our lives had come to an end. He was and always will be my favorite player of all time. The memories he provided for me over a quick five years are ones I will treasure forever. Your old man loves you and is proud of you Jay-Michael.

Matthew Cisco

Chapter 8

Faces of The Mitch

Weston, WV 2007 State Tournament
Sitting front row L-R Melissa Brubeck(Jay-Michaels mom), Carol Cisco(Jay-Michaels "Ganky")
Second row L-R Mark Cisco(Jay-Michael's uncle), Matthew Cisco(Jay-Michaels dad), Dick Griffith (Jay-Michaels great grandfather)

Matthew Cisco

In all my years of being involved with C-K little league baseball, both as a coach and as a player, I have met some interesting people along the way. Some people come and go every four years once their children have finished up their playing time at The Mitch. Others stay around for longer just because they love the game, the environment surrounding Mitch Stadium and the enjoyment of helping the kids learn about the greatest game ever invented. The memories I have of observing these people are ones that I will remember forever. Some of the memories are good and some are bad. The good memories far outweigh the bad ones though. Things that other people may forget or not even notice are the things that I take in and remember.

I remember sitting in the press box and watching the game that was going on before ours. I walked up to the bench and sat down next to Jack Hardin. Mr. Hardin used to be a reporter for our local newspaper and, like many grandfathers, now spent his days watching his grandkids play on such a beautiful ball field. It was a hot day that afternoon and he decided to sit in the press box so he could stay out of the sun. As I said, he was there to watch his grandson who played for the C-K Reds. I sat down and said hello to Mr. Hardin. We sat there for about five minutes and talked about the game that we were watching. It was going to be one of those little league games that would be ended only by a time limit so we had plenty of time to talk. As the conversation wore on I realized I was sitting next to a man that had seen our community grow and change in many different ways. "This all used to be a golf course Matthew. Did you know that?" asked Mr. Hardin. "The little league field used to be a few blocks down off of Rt. 60", he said. I've always enjoyed talking with people from "the greatest generation". The changes they have seen and been a part of in their lifetime had always fascinated me. As I was sitting there I recalled that my grandfather had once told me that Mr. Hardin reported on the Marshall University plane crash in 1970. That crash claimed the lives of almost the entire team and coaching staff. All on board the plane perished. Many of the supporters that were on the plane were known by my grandfather. As a child I remember hearing stories about all of these people and what a big loss it was to the city of Huntington. I'm always fearful of asking about traumatic events in people's lives if they were involved in it. Sometimes people don't like to talk about such things no matter how long a time has passed. So hesitantly I asked Mr. Hardin about his take on the Marshall crash. It was as if a transformation came over his face. Two seconds earlier we were laughing about baseball. I could only imagine that he had taken himself back to November, 14th 1970. I had heard the stories growing up as a child in Kenova. I had read articles, watched documentaries and the "We Are Marshall" movie. None of them took me back to that time the way Mr. Hardin's accounts did. He put me there on the rainy hillside on that fateful evening. I could almost sense the awe he must've felt at seeing such total devastation. He told me he didn't realize it was "our" plane at first. Mr. Hardin was the first reporter to arrive on the scene. He said that he found a wallet lying on the ground that had identification in it. He contacted another reporter for the paper and asked about the name and that reporter said he was a player for Marshall. It was then he realized that it was, in fact, the plane carrying the Marshall University football team home from a game at East Carolina. The way he described not only the horror of realizing it was Marshall's plane but the realization that nobody was alive left me with a greater appreciation of those that had died and for those that followed after. We talked about that tragedy for about another 10 minutes until he slowly guided the conversation back to happier topics of discussion. I could tell that Mr. Hardin was finished reliving that horrible night as I'm sure he's had to do each time he is asked to tell the story. Besides, all is meant to be rosy at The Mitch on game day.

106

Matthew Cisco

Had Dale is another in the line of lifetime supporters of C-K little league baseball. Mr. Dale is an elderly man slowed by age and a voice that has grown softer as the years have passed by. I still say no other person can say my name as sweet as Mr. Dale does. There is something about the way Mr. Dale says "Hello Matthew" that makes you just want to sit down next to him and talk for as long as he will let you. Every so often, and especially during tournament time, you can see Mr. Dale sitting in the second row just behind home plate on the third base side. It was the second day of the 2008 Tournament of Champions. It was around noon that day and we were drying out from a light rain in the morning. Anyone will tell you that light rain on a hot summer day just makes things miserable but there was Mr. Dale taking in a game at The Mitch. None of his family was playing in the game. His only tie being his love of the game and community. I walked next to the press box and saw Mr. Dale sitting there by himself. The sun was almost on top of the field and it was blistering hot. I started to go up to him and I could see that he was sweating buckets. I walked into the concession stand and grabbed an umbrella and went to sit next to him. "Hello Matthew", said Mr. Dale. "How are you Mr. Dale? I brought you an umbrella to give you some shade", I replied. "Aw, thank you Matthew. That was very nice of you" he said. A funny thing happened though. Mr. Dale never reached for the umbrella. Was I supposed to lay it next to him? I didn't know what to do. I had signed up to work in the concession stand for that game and had to get back in there. "How's your mom and granddad" he asked. "They're both doing fine Mr. Dale", I said back to him. As I was getting ready to leave I placed the umbrella next to him and he looked at me with sweat dripping off his head and asked, "How come you don't umpire this tournament anymore? I enjoyed watching you. You reminded me of your father when he umpired." To heck with the concession stand. I slid open the umbrella and held it over Mr. Dale for the next hour and a half. I left only once to get me something to drink because the umbrella wasn't big enough for the both of us and I was melting away to nothing. We sat and talked about my dad and all his recollections of my family and about how the little league game had changed over the years. He talked about the absurdity of not allowing the kids to have an "on-deck" spot on the field. He talked about how kids should still be allowed to put donuts on their bats and how they should ban the curveball from little league. I talked with him about Mrs. Dale and how she was my favorite teacher in all my years of school. Both of them are kind and caring people. As the game wore on so did my arm that was holding the umbrella. After the second inning it would cramp up at least twice an inning. I would take my left hand and place it under my right elbow to help support my arm while keeping Mr. Dale protected from the sun. Surely he would notice my struggle at some point and say that it was ok for me to set the umbrella down. That time never came. By the time the end of the game was in sight my right bicep was about two inches bigger than my left one. I had sweat out almost all of the vital water that my body desperately craved and I had sustained a little sunburn on the right side of my face and neck. I had successfully prevented Mr. Dale from getting third degree burns though and helped cool him down a degree or two. My reward was far greater. I shared in an almost two hour experience with a kindhearted man that I will remember forever.

In all my years of coaching at The Mitch I have seen other coaches come and go. Some of them I found myself wondering who it was that told them they would be a good coach. The majority of coaches coach because they have sons on the team and after their son has played his four years they both move on. There are few that coach that don't have their own children playing. Mick is one such coach. I have always admired the time he has put into teaching these kids about the game of baseball all while taking time away from his own family. The only battles that Mick and I had during

108

my time of coaching with him was the length of practices. I think if he were able to get away with it he would practice the boys five hours a day.

There are some coaches that make it fun when you umpire their games and there have been others that you dread when you find out you are scheduled to call their game. I've been impacted, both good and bad, by many coaches over the years at Mitch Stadium. Even the limited bad experiences that I have had helped make me into a better coach, parent, and umpire during my stay. Very rarely, if ever, has a child impressed me to the point that I had to take a step back and ask myself, "Did he really just do that?" That was until the last game of the 2007 regular season.

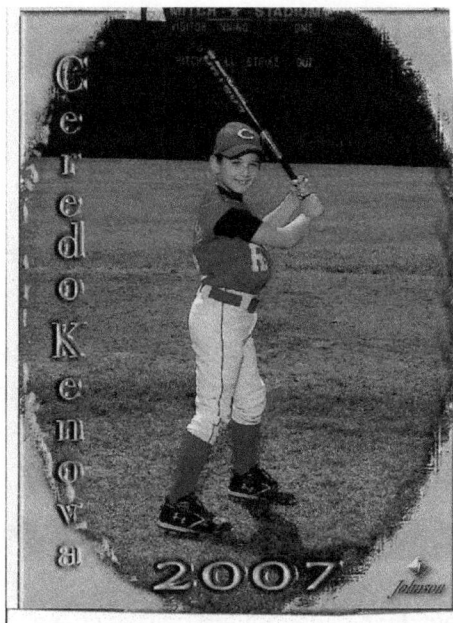

Daniel Rutherford

It was a "meaningless" game between the Reds and the Pirates. It was meaningless in the sense that nothing was to be lost or gained by who won or lost. Both the Reds and the Pirates decided they would pitch kids that normally didn't get to pitch. I was umpiring all the bases that day and I knew I was in for a long one. It seemed the Red's brought in an endless supply of pitching sometimes twice an inning. If I didn't know any better I would've thought they called some of the minor league kids up to pitch to help give you a sense of how many pitching changes were made. By the top of the fifth inning the Pirates had the game well in hand with no chance of losing. That's when Hannah Meade stepped up to the plate. Hannah is the daughter of Pirates coach Barry Meade. She had decided to play baseball for her dad that year and had gone the entire season without even sniffing a hit. "Stay in the box and swing Hannah", Barry would encourage her. Hannah would always seem to hop out of the box even if the pitch was on the outside corner. Strikes one and two came with Hannah hopping out of the box on each pitch. To her credit, though, she swung the bat as she was jumping out of the box. "Come on Hannah, stay in the box", yelled Barry. You could hear it in Barry's voice. He knew this was her one and only year of playing baseball. He knew that this was her last ever at bat. He knew that his daughter was one pitch away from never getting a hit. The next pitch came and I could see Hannah attempting to bail out once again. However, it's as if there was some type of force that wouldn't allow her to do it. She swung the bat and made contact with the ball. She had the misfortune though of hitting it right to the shortstop who then threw it to the best player on the Reds, first baseman Daniel Rutherford. Hannah sprinted out of the box and ran with everything she had. "Run Hannah, RUN", yelled Barry coaching from the first base box. All of the Pirates fans were going crazy with excitement and all cheering on Hannah to run fast. Daniel caught the ball which was a perfect throw to first base. As most umpires do, I looked for Hannah's foot to hit the bag and listened for the smack of the glove catching the ball. As I was preparing myself for the call a hush fell over Mitch Stadium like none ever before. I was watching the bag and listening for the ball to be caught. SMACK! The ball was caught and Hannah's foot was still about 2 feet from the bag. "Saaaaaaaaaaaafe", I screamed while doing the Big Arn dance to

110

really sell the call. I heard some cat calls coming from the Red's dugout. I decided to let it go since I didn't know those coaches seeing how the regular coach was on vacation at the time. I looked at Barry and he winked and nodded his head at me as if to say "Thank you". I was feeling really good about myself even though I was getting heckled from the opposing dugout. I had just been partially responsible for creating a cherished memory between father and daughter. I stood there and watched a father give his daughter a hug and observed a smile on both of their faces that was priceless. This feeling of "I'm the sweetest person on earth" was short lived though as the catcalls continued as I walked behind second base to take position for the next batter. Again, I didn't want to cheapen the moment by calling time and addressing this behavior so I kept on letting it go. As I reached my spot behind the second base bag I looked back at Daniel Rutherford, the nine year old first baseman for the Red's. He just had this grin on his face. It's as if baseball etiquette was just bred into this boy. I thought to myself that it was obvious this boy thought I blew the call and I was impressed on how he handled it. By him just grinning he was giving his opinion to me without saying a word. At such a young age he had already mastered the art of disagreeing with an umpire without showing him up. What impressed me the most happened in the following inning. Daniel came to the plate. As usual he got into his left handed stance and swung away with that beautiful lefty swing that I had tried to force on my son when he was a baby. Daniel ripped a shot to left center field and slid safely into second base. He looked up at me and signaled for time. I approached him to congratulate him on a nice hit and met him at the second base bag at the same time Caleb Meade got there. Caleb is Hannah's older brother and the very same fire baller that I talked about earlier. "Why did you call Hannah safe Matt? You know very well that she was out by a mile" he said to me. I didn't even have a chance to reply when Daniel said, "I don't know what you're talking about Caleb or what game you are watching. It was obvious to me that she beat the throw because I didn't even say a word to him about it." I took a step back and had a quick reflection on Hannah's "hit". Daniel knew she was out and knew I made the incorrect call yet he is standing here and telling Caleb that she beat the throw? I was getting cat calls from grown up's and receiving affirmation from a nine year old child. What's wrong with this picture? In a game that was well out of hand and already decided a nine year old child was able to understand why I made the call that I did yet grown up's missed its meaning entirely? After the game was over I went into the concession stand and got myself a Gatorade. I leaned up against the sink and started to think about what all had just occurred. The Pirates had just destroyed the Red's yet all I could think about was Hannah's "hit" and my meeting at second base with Caleb and Daniel.

I left the concession stand and headed toward the press box to share my story with all that were sitting in there. As I reached the top of the stairs I could hear the substitute coach inside talking about how my call at first base had cost them the game. Without wanting to cause a scene I turned around and walked back down the steps. I went up to about three people until I was successful in getting the phone number of Daniels dad, Dave. He was unable to attend the game that day and I felt it was important that I give him the true version of the story before he heard it from someone else. I told him all about Hannah's play at first base and also about Daniel's reaction to it. "I just wanted to let you know Dave that you have yourself a great kid that is able to understand the bigger picture better than some adults", I told him. "I know I do Matt and thank you for calling me and telling me that", Dave replied.

In all my years of coaching at The Mitch I have been influenced the most by two different coaches, Dan Brody and Scott Milum. Both of these men have been vilified for one reason or the other. The normal complaint on Dan is that he is too loud which some parents interpret as Dan being mean

112

to the kids. I try to explain to them that I say the same things Dan does except in a softer tone. What people don't see however, is Dan in the batting cage. With the rare exception, Dan has thrown batting practice to every kid I have ever coached without missing a beat. I challenge all parents to throw batting practice to thirteen kids, day in and day out, in the heat of the summer.

Scott and Chandler Milum

The one I pattern my coaching style after the most is Scott Milum. I often joke with Scott that I am the only one in all of C-K that likes him. I've never really understood why he gets such a bad rap. The only thing I can think of is how he coached his own sons. I've watched him coach his sons, Chase and Chandler, over the years and he was hard on both of them. Like I said before though, I don't ever judge the way a coach handles his players because all the kids can't be handled the same way. It just so happened that his boys responded better to that brand of coaching. From the outside

113

looking in most parents probably think Scott is mean to them. I'm sure if you ask most of the kids that played for Scott they will tell you that they enjoyed the experience. I think the best way to describe Scott is to compare him to the fictional head coach of the Bad News Bears, Morris Buttermaker. Granted, Scott doesn't drink beer in the dugout or soak a pitchers arm in a bucket of iced beer but he does share other endearing qualities. The biggest one being that most of the parents seem to complain about him yet all the kids on the team grow to love him. To this day you have a good chance of driving by Mitch Stadium and seeing Scott throw batting practice to his son Chandler. He's not one of these types of parents that spend enormous amounts of money by taking his kids to hitting clinics. He doesn't swear by the fact that his boy's are going to be major leaguers one day. He wants his kids to be better though. If his kids take the field he wants them to play at their absolute best. Is there something wrong with that? I would be willing to bet you that Chandler is the one that pesters him about going to the field all the time. Scott has also never been outmatched when it comes to the well being of all little league players. I have seen Scott embrace kids that no other team would pick up just so that kid could experience playing little league baseball. I have seen him with an empty look in his eyes when he has confronted someone that he thinks has wronged a child. I've stepped between him and someone he thinks has undermined a child's opportunity to be able to play little league not knowing if I was going to be unknowingly punched in the altercation. He is almost too loyal to the kids if there is such a thing. Loyalty isn't a bad fault to have though.

At the start of the 2008 preseason Jay-Michael and I drove by the field and saw Scott pitching to Chandler. We got out and watched for a little bit and Scott asked Jay-Michael if he wanted to go in the outfield to shag fly balls. Jay-Michael and I went out on the field and watched as Scott threw what seemed like 100 pitches to Chandler. After his round was done Scott

114

looked at me and asked if I wanted to pitch some to Jay-Michael. "You're going to hit you one this year Jay-Michael", Scott said to him. My boy just grinned and stepped into the box as I toed the rubber. After about five pitches and two bloop hits to center field Scott looked at me and said, "How do you ever expect your kid to hit homeruns when you throw batting practice like that? Get off the mound." Jay-Michael just chuckled and I walked back behind the bag at second. I've always felt that Jay-Michael gets some sort of morbid pleasure out of seeing me put in my place by someone. Well, I must admit that I could tell he was more relaxed now that Scott was throwing to him. Scott's first pitch resulted in a rocket line drive down the third base line. His next pitch was hit out of the park over the right centerfield fence. "That's how you throw batting practice. You better go get your boy's ball", Scott said. I hopped over the brick wall in foul territory down the right field line. I felt like Edwin Moses hurdling over that wall. As I landed on the other side I got a quick reminder that I wasn't him buy the burning pain of ripping a chunk of skin off of my shin as I scaled the wall. It was pain well worth it though and my son was on cloud nine. Never have I heard Scott utter a foul word about a kid in little league. He can talk trash with the young kids better than anyone and they always end up walking away smiling. More often than not he greets my son with a playful headlock and a rake of the knuckles across his head. Scott does have a harsh exterior that people sometimes have trouble seeing past. He is your basic old school type of coach that doesn't follow along with the politically correct ways of doing things. My base running style of coaching and ways of joking with my kids on the team are a direct influence of Scott's ways of doing things. Had he been in the dugout during my sons ten year old state title appearance we would've won the game. I'm just joking Mick, relax.

The Commish, Paul Billups and his daughter Morgan at Rosenblatt
Stadium. An awesome field that doesn't hold a candle to The Mitch.

Matthew Cisco

I would be remiss if I didn't point out what I felt was the main face of C-K Little League Baseball. As I was growing up my favorite team was the Cincinnati Reds. Before I was born they played at Crosley Field. In my youth they played in Riverfront Stadium. As I got older the name of the stadium changed to Cinergy Field. After a few years of playing at Cinergy Field they blew up the stadium after a new park was built and they named that park Great American. My point is this. Elmer Mitchell spent many decades of his life volunteering his time to the 1000's of kids that played baseball at C-K. He spent countless years coaching and even more time spent getting the field ready to play. I've always been one to respect those that came before me. Let us always remember those that gave so freely of their time for the benefit of others.

With that said though, this isn't the field that I played on. The field that I played on was made of spotty grass and just plain dirt. Heck, one year I played at C-K the dirt was this grey looking color that I still have failed to get identified. I remember my mother hated it the most because getting that stuff out of my pants was almost impossible. Mitch and all the other volunteers did the best with what they had but, this isn't the same field anymore. Gone are the flat walk in dugouts with rickety chain mesh fencing and termite ravaged bat racks. Gone are the swinging gates that were always off the hinges that you had to open to get into the dugouts. Gone is the scoreboard whose bulbs were mostly burnt out. If it was up to me, and I know some people might disagree with me, I would name this field Paul Billups Park.

The field that is here now is a direct result of the leadership shown by the commissioner of C-K Little League baseball, Paul Billups. He has been the one to oversee all these changes often facing behind the back criticism along the way. Paul has been the one that has rallied the community

117

together to make these changes possible. He has been the one that has convinced local companies to be generous with their time and money in the creation of this field of dreams. I don't take away one bead of sweat that has been spent by the countless volunteers that have given their time in the reclamation of Mitch Stadium but had it not been for Paul Billups that reclamation would've never occurred.

He played the key role in the creation of The Tournament of Champions. Before this tournament, all-star play ended at the state level for those 9-10 years of age. Paul convinced those in Williamsport to allow him to host this tournament for 9-10 year old state champions from all around the eastern United States. Under his leadership other districts have built new and improved fields. Coincidence? He has transformed your average run of the mill little league field into a field that should receive landmark status. A field that has seen state tournaments, tournament of state champions, and in 2009 it will be hosting the 12 year old regional final with the winner going on to play in the Little League World Series. I can't believe that The Mitch will be televised on national television. The event I enjoyed the most over the years was the Wooden Bat Classic. Paul helped by getting the bats supplied to the league so a handful of lucky teams got to experience what it felt like to play with wooden bats. His whole mode of thinking I'm sure was that a group of boys got to use wooden bats just like the big leaguers and play on a field of major league proportion on a little league scale. What's neat about "The Commish" is his love for the game. He is a purist that feels that baseball should only be played one way and it should be respected by all. Once during the season, when my son's hair became too long he received a letter from Paul on how they were going to resolve this issue. Jay-Michael never cut his hair during the regular season but promised if they won the district in all-stars he would stand on home plate at The Mitch and let his mother take the clippers to his hair. This idea I'm sure was planted in his head by the letter he had received. We won the

118

district that year and Jay-Michael stayed true to his word. For some reason I think the boys on the team were more excited about seeing Jay-Michael getting his hair chopped off than they were of actually winning.

 The majority of drafts I've been a part of have been held at Paul's house. He always seemed to make a big production out of it which always made it more fun for the coaches involved. It was more fun when the drafting process involved coaches bidding on players instead of picking in order. "Ok, little "Johnny" hails from Kenova. A nine year old boy with all the tools and has the ability to help any team instantly. I'll start the bidding at 5,000" he would say. He is always about the theatrics. Theatrics in the game? Charismatic players and umpires? You should be getting the standards that I subscribe to by now. Paul's entire goal is to make the little league experience an enjoyable one for all the kids that come through C-K Little League. He has stressed that to all the coaches. To all the coaches and umpires that come here to participate in post season play he will make that the focal point. He points out that the majority of the kids that play in the Tournament of Champions will never play at a higher level of baseball and that we should make this experience as enjoyable as possible for them. People from other districts always seem to show up during tournament time to "assist" Paul with running the tournament. Some may say it's more like riding the coat tails of another but I will remain happy and say that they are just lending a helping hand. Anyone that knows anything about Mitch Stadium and the tournament it holds will know that Paul Billups and C-K Little League are the reason and not those in surrounding districts that show up when the lights are at their brightest.
 As I've said before there are people from Indiana, North Carolina and so on that have driven here just to be a part of the Tournament of Champions experience without having a connection to any team. It's truly a wonderful event that a select few get to experience. This year Paul had led the effort in rebuilding The Mitch yet again by tearing down and replacing the old

bleachers and press box. As I said, it takes a special person to convince companies to give of their money and time without pause and to lead a large number of volunteers to work on the renovations until the wee hours of the morning. I'm sure that Paul would disagree with some of the things I have said about him and some of my views on those around him. "Matthew, you can't say that" or "Matthew you can't do that" are the two things I often hear from Paul. He almost has a disappointed fatherly tone when he talks to me about things he feels I have done wrong. When he feels that I am right about something though, he will support me regardless of who it offends. I think the best thing I can say about Paul is that he appreciates those that appreciate the game. He appreciates those at The Mitch that really put the time in to make it what it is instead of those that show up right before the first pitch of the tournament. Yet, knowing Paul, he'd give them credit too.

As I started writing this chapter I came to the realization that the overwhelming memories I have involved my family. Mostly they center around the father and son relationship that I had with my dad and that type of relationship he helped me forge with my son. It made me think that it was so much more than that. Jay-Michael's uncle Stevie served in Iraq with the United States Army. In the outfield of The Mitch are signs with advertising on it paid for by the local companies. During the year that Stevie was gone I wanted to have a sign made in his honor so all that came would see his name and know what he was doing for our country. I was unable to afford the price of the sign though yet it somehow made its way into the outfield. During that year, before the start of each game I would point that sign out to our boys and stress to them that it was people like Stevie that made playing that game possible. I'm sure that message fell on the deaf ears of children but it was one I felt important to pass along.

Another person was my grandfather, Dick Griffith. Here was a man in his

Matthew Cisco

90's that would come to watch his great grandson play in a game on a 100 degree day. His body so frail that even on such a hot day he would have to wear a jacket to stay warm. He could only probably see to home plate but wanted to be there anyway if just for the experience. My grandfather was never really the "I love you" type of grandfather. My grandmother was the complete opposite. She would shower me with kisses regardless if I had a great game or not. She would always find a reason to brag on me. Granddad showed his love by just being there. Come hell or high water he would be at his great grandkids games and would always have a recommendation as I walked passed him while I was coaching. His biggest peeve was kids that didn't run on and off the field. "You get them to run on and off the field Matthew and it will shave 30 minutes off the game", he would always say to me.

Beside him would sit my mother. She would just sit and nod at everything granddad had to say. There would be times I knew I would hear it from him as I walked by and I would pretend to be looking at something else and she would catch me every time, "Matthew, come here. Your granddad wants to tell you something", she would say even though she knew I had already heard the same message from him four times prior. I've no doubt that she thinks he was the wisest man she had ever known. She's probably right too. The love she showed for him by making me endure the same message at the end of each inning was priceless.

My Granddad passed away this spring. You'll never be able to convince me otherwise that one of the reasons he lived as long as he did was so he would be able to watch Jay-Michael play his games. When Jay-Michael was nine years old he played in a basketball tournament in Beckley, West Virginia. It's an almost two hour drive from Kenova and has become a sort of mini vacation for the kids and their families. This annual tournament has always been a big deal in our area. Very rarely does a team from little old

My Life at The Mitch: A Little League Baseball Story

Ceredo-Kenova do well in the tournament. This one year however our boy's found themselves in the championship game. There to make the trip, just like every other state tournament that Jay-Michael played in was my Granddad. On the eve of the championship game he became ill and had to be taken to the hospital. He had a blockage in his stomach. It was a touchy situation for awhile especially for a man his age. The possibility of dying, no matter how unlikely, was a reality if not treated properly. Granddad had to miss Jay-Michael and his team win the Beckley tournament. My mother also had to miss the game so she could sit in the hospital with "daddy." Granddad was more ill at the fact of missing his great grandson play in the title game than by the blockage in his stomach. He was the most stubborn man I have ever known and I mean that in the best way possible. He was a man of the greatest generation. He appreciated the little things in life but from my point of view was somewhat hardened by what all he in his generation had to endure. However, I'd never seen him as soft as when he was around my boy. Jay-Michael could've played a game in Siberia and you can bet that my granddad would be there in the front row cheering for his great grandson and hollering at the boys to run off the field. He never had to play there though. My son had the pleasure of playing at The Mitch and there for almost every game was Dick Griffith, my grandfather.

Then I would look upward into the press box and there would sit my Aunt Jane keeping the score. I liken her to a female version of Paul Billups. She truly loves the game of baseball and all the little stories and legends that come with it. She would echo many of the same things that Paul would say to the kids only scaring them a little more along the way. It was truly a magical site. Three generations of one family always at the field to watch my son play and each one calling him by a different name. "Nice hit Jay", it had to be granddad. Granddad for some reason always refused to say Jay-Michael and just cut it short and called him Jay. "Great job Jay-

122

Michael", that would be my mom and Jay-Michaels "Ganky". "Great hit Bubby", would be the cries you would hear from his mother and I. "Way to go Shoeless", my Aunt Jane would yell from the press box.

So at a game would be myself, Melissa, my granddad, my mother, and my aunt. They were all there to root on Jay-Michael and Mason. Little League baseball is truly about family and the memories that family can share. When I sometimes find myself alone on the field during a game I tend to look upward from time to time. I catch myself daydreaming about my granny and my dad. Two huge people in my life that didn't live long enough to see Jay-Michael play little league ball. I wonder what dad would've done after Jay-Michael hit his grand slam in the district tournament. How would granny have teased me that my son was able to hit a homerun in the state tournament and I never could? I wonder how much money she would've offered Jay-Michael to hit a homerun for her. I wonder how she would've loved on Jay-Michael even after a bad game and I wondered about how dad would get on me for being too rough on his "little buddy." Would Jay-Michael still think it was cool to ride on a riding lawn mower to a game? I always seemed to come up with the same answers and I will pass them along to you.

Enjoy the ones that are still here. Enjoy the time your children are in little league because it will be over before you know it. Sure they will move on to Babe Ruth or Cal Ripken ball but nothing can replace the experience and innocence of little league baseball. When your son or the kid you coach makes an error or a dumb play, so what, they are after all kids. In the words of my father, "When they start getting paid to play then you can call them names." Coaches, when an umpire makes a bad call you can question it. This doesn't mean you can make a fool out of yourself. The umpires are being paid with water every inning or so and your win total will not ensure that you will be called up to manage pro ball. The most important thing I can stress is to the parents. I realize that a lot of people miss games due to work. If there is a day that you aren't working but just don't feel up to sitting at the park, go anyway. Before you know it that time in your child's life will be over. My son will never run the bases of Mitch Stadium again. My time at The Mitch was precious and it ended all too soon. Grasp it and live every moment of your child's little league experience to the fullest. Ignore nobody. Talk with people at the ball games and build relationships. As for people like me, don't ignore the sound advice from a grandfather even if just once. Let them say it every inning if they want to. I would give anything to have my Granddad get on me one more time about getting my boys to run off the field. I would love to have my dad and granny around to spoil my son with accolades. As clichéd as it sounds though, they were. Every time I looked to the sky a breeze would always seem to blow. This would signal to me that they had the best seat in the house.

Matthew Cisco

To all of my family that supported Jay-Michael and I through this fast, five year journey we thank you. Little League sports are about family, that's it. It doesn't matter if you are the starting pitcher for the all-star team or the kid that sat beside me in the dugout on opening day spitting seeds. All deserve those same types of memories that I have tried to share with you. I'm sure most people at other little league fields across the land can relate to some of the stories I have talked about in this book. Mine just happened to take place in the wonderful, little town of Kenova, West Virginia at the magical stadium simply known as The Mitch.

www.ingramcontent.com/pod-product-compliance
Lightning Source LLC
LaVergne TN
LVHW091308080426
835510LV00007B/423